I0825383

HOW TO GET A RETURN ON FAILURE

HOW TO GET A RETURN ON FAILURE

Fail Smarter—Return Stronger

JOHN C. MAXWELL

Forbes | Books

Published by Forbes Books, Charleston, South Carolina.
An imprint of Advantage Media Group.

Printed in the United States of America.

10 9 8 7 6 5 4 3 2 1

ISBN: 979-8-88750-795-8 (Hardcover)
ISBN: 979-8-88750-796-5 (eBook)

Library of Congress Control Number: Applied

Cover design by Matthew Morse.
Layout design by Lance Buckley.

Since 1917, Forbes has remained steadfast in its mission to serve as the defining voice of entrepreneurial capitalism. Forbes Books, launched in 2016 through a partnership with Advantage Media, furthers that aim by helping business and thought leaders bring their stories, passion, and knowledge to the forefront in custom books. Opinions expressed by Forbes Books authors are their own. To be considered for publication, please visit **books.Forbes.com**.

10-09-2025 4:23

THIS BOOK IS DEDICATED TO STEVE MILLER.

You have been steadfast and courageous
in the face of life's great challenges and tragedies.
Few people I know have been better at
treating defeat as an investment in a better future.
You always get a positive return on failure.
Thank you for being a faithful friend to me and to EQUIP.

Contents

Acknowledgments ix

Introduction 1

1. See Failure as an Investment in Your Future 3
2. Keep Success and Failure Together 21
3. To Get Over Failure, Get Over Yourself 39
4. Use Failure to Make Yourself Better 59
5. Embrace the Value of Hard 77
6. Practice the Cycle of Improvement 99
7. Learn the Difference Between Good Misses and Bad Misses 117
8. Lead Others Through Failure 137
9. The Future Favors the Bold 157

About the Author 161

Endnotes 163

Acknowledgments

I want to say thank you to Charlie Wetzel, Jared Cagle, and Erin Miller, who assisted me with thinking through and writing this book. I also want to thank the people in my organizations who support me. You all add incredible value to me, which allows me to add value to others. Together, we're making a difference!

Introduction

What separates successful people from unsuccessful people? I'm sure you've thought about it. Do they start life with greater advantages: money, education, upbringing? Have they received greater and better opportunities than others? Are they smarter? Are they simply luckier?

Many of those factors certainly come into play. But I can tell you this: The difference is *not* the avoidance of failure. Successful people fail as often as unsuccessful people. In fact, they often fail more. The difference is that they know how to deal with failure in a positive way, so positive that they get a positive return on failure—an ROI. They think differently, they process failure differently, they act differently, and as a result, they get different results. If you want to be as successful as you can be and reach your full potential, you need to learn how to get a return on failure. The good news is that you can. And I can teach you.

As you read this book, I will teach you how to:

- See Failure as an Investment in Your Future,
- Keep Success and Failure Together,
- Get Over Failure by Getting Over Yourself,
- Use Failure to Make Yourself Better,
- Embrace the Value of Hard,
- Practice the Cycle of Improvement,

- Learn the Difference Between Good Misses and Bad Misses, and
- Lead Others Through Failure.

If you do all of these things, you will be able to fail smarter and return stronger. And you will help the people you lead to do the same. You will still fail, but you will be able to get a return on failure. So let's get started.

1

See Failure as an Investment in Your Future

Failure! What does that word do to you when you hear it? What's its impact? Does it make you shudder or smile? Does it cause you to retreat or advance? If you're like most people, you never want that word applied to you, and you will do everything you can to avoid failing.

But what if that's a wrong way of thinking? What if failure is actually *necessary* for you to become successful, to reach your full potential? What if you could learn to not only appreciate failure but use it to your benefit? What if you could learn to profit from nearly every loss you experience in life and get a return on failure—like an investment?

Let me tell you, not only is that possible, but it's actually the best way forward in life. The most successful people succeed because they deal with failure positively. They *gain* from it. Their approach to failure strengthens the foundation of their lives and makes it possible for them to build more substantial and significant success. They consistently receive an ROI on their mistakes and missteps.

Max De Pree said, "The first responsibility of a leader is to define reality."[1] As a veteran leader with a lot of life experience, I want to help you by defining the reality of failure: Failure will always be a part of your life. You cannot avoid it. But you *can* leverage it to create a better future for yourself. When you do that, it will separate you from the people who let failure stop or defeat them.

APPRECIATE WHAT YOU CAN'T AVOID

The first step toward seeing failure as an investment in your future is to learn to appreciate failure instead of trying to avoid it. If you look up *appreciation*, you'll find that it has three basic meanings:

> 1 the act or fact of appreciating; specifically, *a)* proper estimation or enjoyment *b)* grateful recognition, as of a favor *c)* sensitive awareness or enjoyment, as of art 2 a judgment or evaluation 3 a rise in value or price: opposed to depreciation[2]

Appreciating failure means properly estimating the advantages it brings as you learn from it. It means recognizing the opportunities failure gives you to develop character and hone new skills. It means becoming aware of the places you need to grow. It means understanding how it improves your judgment and evaluative skills as you grow from it. It means recognizing that your positive experience of dealing with failure makes you more valuable. Appreciating failure makes you less fearful of taking risks. The ability to deal with failure opens doors to the exploration of new territory and a life of greater potential. And know this: Appreciation is a gift you must choose for yourself. But it is also a discipline you must practice. It takes intentionality.

HOW TO PREPARE YOURSELF TO FAIL WELL

Appreciation instead of apprehension will help you to see failure as an investment in yourself, your growth, and your future. But you must still properly prepare yourself to face failure positively. My mentor John Wooden often said, "When opportunity comes, it's too late to prepare." The same can be said of the need to prepare for failure. To get yourself ready, here are seven things I suggest you do.

Appreciation instead of apprehension will help you to see failure as an investment in yourself, your growth, and your future.

1. Expect to Fail

Did you know that nearly a fifth of all businesses in the United States fail in their first year? And more than half fail after five years?[3] That means if you want to become a business owner, you have less than a fifty-fifty shot at making it. Yet very few new business leaders take the possibility of failing into account. And they have no contingency plan in the event they find themselves in trouble.

I'm often amazed at how surprised people are when one of their efforts fails or when they experience a major setback. Why would anyone expect every endeavor to go smoothly or to do every task perfectly? It's impossible. No one succeeds without failing along the way. As human beings, we need to anticipate failing.

When you expect to fail, it softens your fall and shortens your recovery. Charlie Wetzel, my longtime writing partner, used to train in martial arts. When he was training in aikido, he said one of the first things he was taught was how to do a roll. He found out why that was important the first time his sensei threw him. Instead of falling on his face or breaking his wrist by trying to stop his fall, proper technique enabled him to take the throw, roll on his shoulder, and come up onto his feet. Later, at higher levels of training, he learned how to pivot in the air when thrown and land safely on his side.

My favorite story about how anticipating failure can help happened to me and members of my team in 1998 at the end of a five-day book tour. We were flying home and were about to land when our chartered plane was hit with wind shear and suddenly dropped sickeningly toward the ground. But the moment the wheels began to touch the ground, the pilot pushed the throttle hard and thrust the plane back up into the air. It shook all of us, and we thanked God for our pilot's flying skill. He circled and landed smoothly on his second attempt.

After we landed, I asked him, "How did you make such a quick decision to take the plane back up into the air?"

"Oh, that wasn't a quick decision at all," he replied. "I made that decision twenty years ago when I started flying." He explained that as a young pilot, he spent time preparing himself for every potential problem and failure he could imagine while flying a plane. His quick ascent back into the air was his response to that potential failure. With a knowing smile, he said, "There's a greater margin for error in the air than on the ground." In that particular case, his expectation of failure enabled him to prevent it. And for that, we were all very grateful.

2. Practice Self-Compassion

Since we *will* inevitably fail, we need to give ourselves grace and compassion when we do. We need to be kind and understanding toward ourselves. We need to be patient with our struggles and work through them. That is not always easy.

When I let myself down, if I have a difficult time because of it, I remind myself of three truths:

We All Want to Be Valued by Our Best Moments

A lot of us have good days and bad days, experience ups and downs, produce highlights and lowlights. Sometimes, we even have no lights! Nobody wants to be defined by their downs. This is universally true. When I make this point while speaking, I ask the question, "How many of you have ever had a day that you hope nobody ever knows about?" All the people who are honest with themselves raise a hand. I raise both hands because I've had more than my share of days I'm embarrassed by. When I have a bad day, I remind myself, "That's what I did, but that's not who I am."

Even though you have failed, that doesn't mean you are a failure. Show yourself compassion. Give yourself grace and choose to focus on your ups more than your downs.

Nothing Happens TO You—It Happens FOR You

When I experience misses and failures, I often encourage myself with the phrase "Nothing happens *to* you—it happens *for* you," which I heard from my friend Joel Osteen. Why? Because if I think my failures happen *to* me, I start to take on the role of victim. When that happens, I live in my pain. And here's what I've discovered: Hurting people often hurt themselves and others. I don't want to do those things.

Nothing happens to you—it happens for you.

—Joel Osteen

Jamie Kern Lima likes to ask a valuable question: "Do you victim-up or warrior-up?"[4] If I can warrior-up, I believe that all things, good or bad, happen *for* me. That empowers me to see my failures in a positive light, and as a result, I respond to them in a positive way.

That's important to me not only personally but also because I carry the responsibilities of a leader. I can't moan and lead at the same time. People may feel sorry for a victim, but they will never follow one. I need and want to lead. Being honest yet compassionate with myself and looking for the positive in the face of the negative help me to be a better leader.

The High Road Is the Best Road

Your approach to life impacts your approach to failure. Taking the high road in life means you treat yourself, as well as others, with compassion and respect. It means forgiving others. When you do that freely, you are also better able to forgive yourself. But that requires maintaining a high-road mindset. As Martin Luther King, Jr., said, "Forgiveness is not an occasional act; it is a permanent attitude."[5] The high road stretches out longer than a block or two. And taking it has a toll. Forgiving is not forgetting. It's remembering what happened and *choosing* to forgive. Making that choice brings freedom and lightness to your journey. You become able to travel without baggage.

Practicing self-compassion puts you in a better place to deal with failure. It enables you to be your own best friend and encourage yourself. If, as someone said, encouragement is oxygen for the soul, then during the difficult times of overcoming failure, encouragement is life support.

3. Focus on the Big Game Instead of the Blame Game

Music teacher and author Eloise Ristad used to coach musicians to help them experience breakthroughs. She believed people often tried so hard that their effort got in the way of great performance.[6] She often helped them by letting them know it was OK to fail. She wrote:

> When we give ourselves permission to fail, we at the same time give ourselves permission to excel. … We try so hard to succeed, all of us. We try so hard to be good people, to avoid making mistakes. … After all that trying, it is such a luxury to know that it is not only permissible to fail part of the time, but an essential ingredient of being human. And we find that the failing is not failing at all, but merely learning.[7]

To see failure as an investment in your future, you need to stop worrying about the blame game and focus on the big game. The blame game is preoccupied with who is at fault. The big game concentrates on progress and production, which inevitably include both wins and losses. It acknowledges failure as normal. (I share more about this in chapter 2.)

The big game also requires a willingness to try new things, admit both small and large failures, evaluate them, learn from them, and improve. This includes analyzing failures and proactively searching for opportunities to experiment. (I discuss this in chapter 6.) When we keep the big game in mind, the attitude is that we're in the discovery business, and the faster we fail, the faster we discover ways to improve and succeed. In today's complex world, those who identify and learn from failure before others do will succeed. Those who wallow in the blame game will not.

4. Embrace and Live a Positive Life Stance

Psychiatrist Theodore Isaac Rubin said, "The problem is not that there are problems. The problem is expecting otherwise and thinking that having problems is a problem."[8] The same can be said about failures. While we can't change the fact that we will have problems and we will experience failures, we can change our attitude about them. We can embrace a positive life stance.

When I was a boy, my father coached me on having a positive attitude. I was reminded of those teachings many years later during a mentoring session with John Wooden. He said, "Sometimes we get involved in things that we have no control of, and they end up negatively affecting what we do have control over." His observation challenged me to stop trying to eliminate or control the bad and remember to take control of my attitude, not just occasionally but continually, as a life stance. Here's an expression of what that means:

Life is filled with good and bad.

Some of the good and bad I can't control—it's life.

Some of the good and bad will find me.

If I have a positive life stance, the good
and bad will become better.

If I have a negative life stance, the good
and bad will become worse.

Therefore, I choose a positive life stance.

A positive life stance doesn't make my failures disappear, but it does lessen their impact and put them into proper perspective.

5. Reframe Failure

How you think about failure affects how you respond to failure. Positive psychology coach Paula Thompson says failure can be defined as a lack of success or the inability to meet an expectation. When we take that definition to heart, she says:

> We can read too much into failure. Too often, we attach it to our self-worth, self-esteem, and self-acceptance. The

expectation we fail to meet is often our own, or one that we created in our own head.

Most of us don't set out looking to fail at anything. And we especially don't want to be labeled as failures. But maybe that is a mistake.

Failure can be useful. We can learn from it, gain new insights, and do better next time. The right kind of failure moves us closer to our goals.[9]

Is a failure always truly a failure? Is a victory always truly a victory? John Wooden told me he felt very disappointed when his University of California, Los Angeles (UCLA) basketball team won a game that he thought they didn't deserve to win. While his players celebrated on the court, he walked off knowing that practice the next week would be difficult. The win would make it hard for his players to see all the mistakes they made in the game, and they would be less hungry to listen, learn, and change. Coach Wooden said, "In the eyes of the players, the score meant success. In my eyes, the score was misleading." Success that is defined as only hitting the goal needs to be reframed. So does failure that is defined as missing the goal. Both definitions lack perspective.

To reframe failure, Amy C. Edmondson, Novartis Professor of Leadership and Management at the Harvard Business School, suggests that organizations look at the context of failures to better understand why they happened. This opens the door to learning and improving. She places failures in organizations on a spectrum, labeling the preventable failures as "blameworthy" and the most positive failures as "praiseworthy." Here are the types of failures she identifies, starting with the blameworthy and working down to the praiseworthy (with my descriptions)[10]:

BLAMEWORTHY ↔ PRAISEWORTHY	
BLAMEWORTHY	**Deviance:** People choose not to follow established processes or practices.
	Inattention: People inadvertently fail to follow established processes or practices.
	Lack of Ability: People lack the skill, training, or insight to do a job well.
	Process Inadequacy: People with ability follow a faulty or incomplete process.
	Task Challenge: People attempt tasks that are too difficult to be completed correctly every time.
	Process Complexity: People follow a process that breaks down because of exceptions.
	Uncertainty: People take good actions that end in bad results because of unexpected future events.
	Hypothesis Testing: People act to validate the success of an idea or design but fail.
PRAISEWORTHY	**Exploratory Testing:** People fail in an experiment to expand knowledge and investigate possibilities.

When you reframe failure by looking at context—or any other factors, such as history, circumstances, relationships, and so forth—you obtain a bigger and better picture of their causes and remedies. Reframing failure also removes some of the fear of failure and allows you to seize opportunities instead of avoiding them.

6. Find the Benefits of Every Bad Experience

Cartoon character Homer Simpson summed up his philosophy of dealing with failure when he said, "Kids, you tried your best and you failed miserably. The lesson is, never try."[11] If everyone followed that philosophy, we'd still be living in caves, freezing in the winter, and walking to every place we wanted to go. If you want to move forward in life, you can't give up or cover up your failure. To use failure as an investment in your future, you have to find the benefits in every failure and use them to learn and grow.

There's a story that has been all over the internet for a number of years about a farmer and a donkey. It uses humor to teach a wonderful lesson about failure. Just in case you somehow missed it, here it is:

> One day a farmer's donkey fell down into a well. The animal cried piteously for hours as the farmer tried to figure out what to do. Finally, he decided the animal was old, and the well needed to be covered up anyway; it just wasn't worth it to retrieve the donkey.
>
> He invited all his neighbors to come over and help him. They all grabbed a shovel and began to shovel dirt into the well. At first, the donkey realized what was happening and cried horribly. Then to everyone's amazement he quieted down.
>
> A few shovel loads later, the farmer finally looked down the well. He was astonished at what he saw. With each shovel of dirt that hit his back, the donkey was doing something amazing. He would shake it off and take a step up.
>
> As the farmer's neighbors continued to shovel dirt on top of the animal, he would shake it off and take a step up. Pretty

> soon, everyone was amazed as the donkey stepped over the edge of the well and happily trotted off!
>
> Life is going to shovel dirt on you, all kinds of dirt. The trick to getting out of the well is to shake it off and take a step up. Each of our troubles is a steppingstone. We can get out of the deepest wells just by not stopping, never giving up! Shake it off and take a step up. …
>
> The donkey later came back and bit the farmer who had tried to bury him. The gash from the bite got infected and the farmer eventually died in agony from septic shock.
>
> Moral From Today's Lesson: When you do something wrong and try to cover your ass, it always comes back to bite you.[12]

Never try to run from failure or cover it up, or you'll end up like the farmer.

7. Expect Your Failure Investment to Take Time to Pay Off

I've written quite a bit about my desire to see a country transformed by good values before I die. That's why I've launched initiatives using transformation tables in many countries. So far, we've worked in Guatemala, Paraguay, Costa Rica, the Dominican Republic, Papua New Guinea, Panama, and Brazil. We've also begun introducing values-based curricula in many states in the United States. Will all these initiatives succeed? I would love that, but I don't *expect* them to. I know that any time you initiate a new project, the failure rate is high. But I'm not looking for quick victories. I'm on this journey for the long haul. Whenever I find myself or one of these efforts failing, I will do three things:

- I will keep moving.
- I will keep adjusting.
- I will keep believing.

Nothing good happens when we give up. When we keep moving, resources keep coming to us. When we keep trying and adjusting, we find more and better answers. And if we keep believing, we never lose hope. The mission is greater than any failure we might face. And for that reason, we keep making positive investments.

Whenever I find myself or one of these efforts failing, I will do three things: I will keep moving. I will keep adjusting. I will keep believing.

Seeing failure as an investment in a better future not only makes a positive impact on you; it can also positively impact others around you. That was true for one of my heroes, John Wesley. The English preacher was a strong proponent of the abolition of slavery, which he first confronted in 1736 on a trip to Georgia when he visited the United States. After that, the more Wesley learned about slavery, the stronger his conviction that it must be abolished. In 1774, he published "Thoughts Upon Slavery," strongly condemning the practice.

Did Wesley's preaching and writing against slavery stop the practice in his lifetime? No. In that sense, he failed. But his writings influenced many people, including John Newton, a former sea captain and slave trader. Newton, in turn, influenced William Wilberforce, an English politician who was opposed to slavery. Newton convinced Wilberforce to remain in politics and keep fighting for the abolition of slavery. Wesley joined Newton in his encouragement of Wilberforce. In fact, the last letter Wesley wrote in 1791, just six days before his death, was to Wilberforce. He wrote, "O be not weary of well doing! Go on, in the name of God and in the power of his might, till even American slavery (the vilest that ever saw the sun) shall vanish away before it."[13]

For the next forty-two years, Wilberforce and others worked to abolish slavery in England and failed. But they maintained the long view and kept trying. Finally, in 1833, England abolished the slave trade. And in 1865, after a bloody civil war, the United States followed suit.

To receive an ROI on failure, you must maintain the long view too. You need to see personal and professional success in the same way you see financial success. You must give your investment time to grow and compound. Like a financial portfolio, you will experience up days and down days, good years and bad years. Sometimes, your growth will be rapid—other times, painfully slow. But it all adds up. And in the end, failure and success are like two sides of the same coin that can't be separated from each other. I'll explain how that works in the next chapter.

DISCUSSION QUESTIONS

If you're reading this book with a group or as part of a mastermind, use the discussion questions to explore ideas, share insights and struggles, and grow together.

1. What is your earliest childhood memory of failing? How did you know what you did really was a failure? How did it make you feel and how did you respond?
2. In the household where you grew up, how were failures, mistakes, and messes treated?
3. In your experience, how have teachers in schools and leaders at work typically reacted to failures, mistakes, and problems when people make them? Has any authority figure in your past welcomed them and encouraged you to fail?
4. Where do you land on a scale of 1 to 10 where 1 means you try to avoid any situation where you might fail or face trouble and 10 means you'll try anything because you value the experience more than the outcome? How does the score you gave yourself impact your potential for achieving greater success?
5. How can a person develop appreciation for failure instead of feeling apprehension toward it? How good are you at doing that?
6. What is the greatest thing you would attempt to do if you knew you could not fail?
7. If you could change one thing about yourself to make you less failure-averse, what would it be? What is preventing you from making that change?

ACTION STEPS TO SEE FAILURE AS AN INVESTMENT IN YOUR FUTURE

Take these steps from the chapter to get a bigger return on failure in your life:

1. Practice Self-Compassion

Combat your negative feelings about yourself by making a list of your best moments. You have taken good actions, helped other people, and accomplished worthwhile tasks in your life. Write a list of these positive actions. Then the next time you're feeling down because you made a mistake, failed, or stumbled, take out the list and read it to remind yourself of who you are at your best.

2. Stop the Blame Game

Finding who to blame when something goes wrong is not nearly as useful as finding the lesson that can be learned from it. The next time you or your team don't get the desired results from something you're doing, focus your attention on the lesson to be learned, and then make sure everyone involved discusses it to avoid the same problem in the future.

3. Reframe Failure

The next time you experience a problem, review Edmondson's failure spectrum, which runs from Deviance to Exploratory Testing, and determine where your difficulty or actions fall on her scale. Use that to reframe your thinking, learn what went wrong, and determine how to do better next time.

4. Create Your Positive Life Stance

Take some time to write your own positive life stance or statement of positivity. Make it something that captures your values and aspirations. You may want to draw from or be inspired by the list you created while practicing self-compassion. What you write may be very personal and private. Or you may want to carefully craft something you will allow others to read. Either way, the important thing is that it represents you genuinely and is something you aspire to live every day.

2

Keep Success and Failure Together

People often think of success and failure as mortal enemies. Success is the hero of our lives. Failure is the villain. We root for success and keep failure as far away from us as possible. We tell ourselves, "Never fail. Don't mess up. Don't make mistakes." But there's a problem with this. Life doesn't work that way. We should not be thinking about success *versus* failure. Instead, we should be thinking of success *and* failure.

In a poem titled "If—," Rudyard Kipling wrote about what it takes to experience a positive life in which "yours is the Earth and everything that's in it." Touching briefly on success and failure, Kipling calls them "triumph" and "disaster," and his advice is to "treat those two impostors just the same,"[14] meaning we shouldn't let them define our lives. Neither should be given the weight we often assign to them. I love that because no one always succeeds and never fails, nor does anyone always fail and

We should not be thinking about success *versus* failure. Instead, we should be thinking of success *and* failure.

never succeed. Both paths are impossible. Success and failure are present in every person's life, and we should intentionally *keep* them together because it puts us in a better position to get a positive return on failure.

THE DANGERS OF SEPARATING SUCCESS AND FAILURE

If we separate success and failure in our minds and convince ourselves that we can live with one and not the other, we create undesirable barriers to our potential. I will explain what I mean.

Success Alone Creates Overconfidence

Microsoft cofounder Bill Gates said, "Success is a lousy teacher. It seduces smart people into thinking they can't lose."[15] Confidence is good. Self-assurance is necessary for success. But believing you *can't* lose is arrogance. That kind of overconfidence is harmful. Arrogant people don't grow. They don't change when they need to, they take unnecessary risks, and they harm other people.

People who experience great success tend to be less reflective too. Harvard Business School professors Francesca Gino and Gary P. Pisano conducted a study to examine how people react to success and failure. They wrote:

> Students from U.S. universities were asked to work on two decision-making problems. Learning from experience on the first problem could help them perform well on the second. After submitting their solutions to the first problem, the participants were told whether or not they had succeeded. They were then given time to reflect before starting the second problem. Compared with the people

> who failed at the first problem, those who succeeded spent significantly less time reflecting on the strategies they'd used. This had a cost: Those who succeeded on the first task were more likely to fail on the second.[16]

As with John Wooden's players who won without earning it, when we succeed, we can take success for granted. When we experience one success after another, we need to be even more careful because what we're experiencing is merely a winning streak, and all streaks end. When casino gamblers on winning streaks stay at the tables long enough, they start to lose. When I'm playing golf and I shoot great scores for several holes, I know it's only a matter of time until I have a bad hole. That's why I'm grateful there are eighteen of them!

Winning without losing is not possible. Casinos know that. Golfers know that. Sports teams know it. You and I need to know it too. If we work to keep success and failure together, we're more likely to recognize streaks—both positive and negative.

Success Alone Decreases Our Desire to Ask Tough Questions

Another observation made by Gino and Pisano while analyzing the results of their study was that people who succeed tend not to ask themselves *why* questions. The professors called this the failure-to-ask-why syndrome:

> The tendency is to not investigate the causes of good performance systematically. When executives and their teams suffer from this syndrome, they don't ask the tough questions that would help them expand their knowledge or alter their assumptions about how the world works.[17]

Whenever we are confronted with failure, it is natural to ask why, to examine what happened. Unfortunately, we often interpret success as evidence that our existing strategies and practices work, even if we haven't confirmed this to be true. This ignores other variables and blinds us to our need to adjust and improve.

The best leaders and achievers continually ask themselves tough questions—after both wins and losses. My friend Jim Tressel, who was the head football coach at Ohio State University from 2001 to 2010, told me, "I grade and evaluate our winning games as much as I do the ones we lose." He didn't allow his wins—and he had a lot in his career record of 229–79–2—to breed complacency within his coaching staff.[18] No wonder he was elected to the College Football Hall of Fame.

In our organization, we strive to ask tough questions, not only when we fail but also when we succeed. For example, every six months, our company trains Maxwell Leadership certified coaches at a conference in Orlando. I love the culture of our coaching team. A big bright sign over the event's help desk says it all: "The Answer Is Yes!" Our staff has created an atmosphere that is productive, positive, and successful. I believe that's one of the reasons we've become the biggest coaching organization in the world.

When the conference is over, there are a lot of high fives. But our staff also spends hours asking tough questions to try to figure out how to improve the conference. We refuse to allow success to lull us into complacency.

Success Alone Makes Us Unappreciative

If we experience nothing but success, we start to take the positive things in our lives for granted. We *need* the negative to truly appreciate the positive. What makes us appreciate warm, sunny days? Cold, rainy days. What makes us appreciate good health? The days we're ill.

What makes us enjoy victories? Our defeats. Remembering our losses keeps us fighting and staying in the game when we're failing because we still hope to win. That's why Napoleon Hill wrote: "Every adversity brings with it the seed of an equivalent advantage."[19] What does that seed represent? The possibility of victory.

Failure Alone Makes Us Feel Hopeless

As troublesome as success alone may be, continual failure is even worse. Anytime people believe that failure is inevitable, they lose hope. They become depressed. They want to give up. What a terrible place to be. More than anyone else in the world, discouraged people need to keep success and failure together.

I saw an old *Peanuts* comic strip in which Charlie Brown is talking with his friend Linus. "Life is rarely all one way, Charlie Brown," Linus says. "You win a few, and you lose a few!"

"Really," Charlie responds. "Gee, that'd be neat!!"[20]

As someone who was always facing failure, he would have loved to experience even one victory. Why? Because he always struck out. His team always lost. Lucy always pulled away the football at the last second when he tried to kick it. And when he went trick-or-treating, while the other kids got candy, he always got a rock. Even his dog was more popular than he was. What he needed in his life were a few wins. He needed his feelings of failure to be balanced by feelings of success.

THE POWER OF KEEPING FAILURE AND SUCCESS TOGETHER

Whenever failure and success are separated, we lose perspective. I see this often when people attribute their successes to their skills and their failures to bad circumstances. That is not a mature or realistic perspective, and I wonder how anyone can become so delusional. The opposite is just as likely to be true. I know that's been true for me. A lot of the good in my life has come from others, not me. And many of my failures were the result of my poor skills or decisions, not circumstances. I bet that's true for you too.

I'm sure you intuitively understand the value and power of keeping failure and success together, but I want to spend the rest of this chapter emphasizing three important benefits of doing this.

1. Keeping Failure and Success Together Presents a True Picture of Life

It's tempting for us to look at highly successful people and imagine that they don't have to deal with failure, but that's a false picture of life. The truth is that the most successful people have always been shaped and helped by failure. How do I know this? I've talked with hundreds of people at the pinnacle of their careers, from Fortune 100 CEOs to media moguls to famous historians to Hall of Fame coaches to presidents of countries. Often, I've engaged with them at what I call a learning lunch, where I interview them as we dine together. One of the questions I always ask is, "What is the greatest lesson you have ever learned?" While every person's answer is unique, all of their answers have one thing in common. Their greatest lessons *always* come from failure. They credit failure, in great part, for their success. In fact, I have never met anyone whose major success didn't hinge on some past failure they experienced. I believe that's why Albert Einstein said, "Failure is success in progress."[21]

"Failure is success in progress."

—Albert Einstein

In my book *Developing the Leader Within You 2.0*, I wrote about how difficult it is to live an authentic life when we separate failure and success. I encourage leaders to embrace and talk about both with others, because if they try to hide their failures, they come across as phony. And if they try to hide their successes, they lack credibility with others. Genuine people acknowledge both. People who achieve much in life live with both.

I see failure and success like the boundary lines on the two edges of a road. Here's how I describe them in my book:[22]

THE LINE OF FAILURE	THE LINE OF SUCCESS
Weakness	**Strength**
Depresses me	**Impresses me**
I want no one to see	**I want everyone to see**
I want this never	**I want this forever**
Me at my worst	**Me at my best**

Most of the time, we live between those two lines. When people see us on the success line, we have to be careful not to think that is who we really are. We can be like athletes who win a gold medal or a Super Bowl and start to believe they're spectacular all the time at everything they do. That's not reality. We may try to put famous people on a pedestal, but they will surely fall off.

There are also times when we travel along the failure line. We all make mistakes. We all make bad choices. We all fall short. If we believe that's who we are, we won't want to get out of bed. We shouldn't buy into that, either. Both lines—of success and failure—are extremes. We're neither as good as we wish nor as bad as we fear.

My advice to everyone is to travel down the middle of the road because this is what I know: If I go off the road on the failure side, I will feel discouraged. I will become consumed with my mess-ups. If I stay in the success lane, I'll become too comfortable and stop paying close attention to what I'm doing, and I'll stop paying the price to be my best. Either extreme will get me off course. So, I get back to the middle of the road where I'm positive, alert, and responsive to what's happening around me.

To live a life that is authentic, productive, and fulfilling, stay connected to both failure and success. Don't let the pull of one or the other drag you off the road and crash your future.

2. Keeping Failure and Success Together Allows Them to Complement Each Other

Failure and success can complement and strengthen each other if you put them together. Think of it this way. Stretch your arms out wide and imagine that one hand is success and the other is failure. If someone were to push one of your hands down, you'd have a difficult time keeping that arm out straight, wouldn't you? Now, lock your hands together in front of you with your fingers intertwined. If someone were to push down on your hands, you would find it much easier to resist because you would be in a much stronger position. That's what keeping failure and success together is like.

How does failure complement success? What value does it bring? Humility. When we are humbled by failure but don't let it break us, we are better able to maintain a teachable spirit. We become willing to admit that we don't know all the answers. We desire to learn. We become open to accepting feedback from others. And once we've developed humility, even when we win, we can avoid arrogance because we understand it's not all about us. We accept both failure and success with grace.

How does success complement failure? It helps us develop resilience. If we have experienced some success, when we stumble and fall, we recognize that failure doesn't have to be personal or permanent. It helps us know that when we experience tough times and adversity, we can get through them. We develop a spirit of tenacity that helps us rise above difficulties. I love the way Thomas Edison expressed this idea: "I've had a lot of success with failure."[23]

"I've had a lot of success with failure."

—THOMAS EDISON

One of the toughest years I experienced in my life was 1980. At the time, it felt like a failure year. Why? First, I felt a calling to teach leadership to a larger audience, and I realized I would not be able to do that effectively in the position I held. I loved the people I led, but I felt compelled to pursue my potential, so I left that position. My family and I moved to a city we didn't like, and I took a new job that didn't fit me. On top of that, most of my peers, who remained comfortably in the organization I had left, criticized my decision, which made me sad.

In my new role, I broke ground, worked to spread my wings, and trained leaders in several states. But the changes I was making made people in my new organization uneasy. They felt that I was rocking the boat too much, so I was always experiencing resistance. In addition, my new role caused me to travel so much that I missed my wife, Margaret, and my two young children. It was like a perfect storm in my life.

How did I get through such a difficult year? By keeping success close to me. Every day, I reminded myself of why I had made the decision to move. Every day, I reminded myself, "It's not what happens *to* me; it's what happens *in* me that counts." Every day, I did what I knew was right, even though I often didn't feel like doing it. Every day, I celebrated little wins to find encouragement in the journey. Every day, I sought joy in adding value to others. Every day, I thought about the big picture of who I wanted to become, not just the bad picture of what I was going through. I placed any success I found alongside every failure because I believed that, one day, I would receive an ROI on that failure.

Several great things came out of that difficult season. First, I proved to myself that the leadership principles I was teaching were applicable to a much larger and more diverse audience than I had previously reached. Second, the success I experienced training leaders opened the door for my next leadership position in San Diego—at a church and in a city I loved. Finally, that difficult year planted in me the idea for a book I wrote many years later called *Today Matters*. In that book, which Margaret says represents who I am better than any other, I teach what I call my daily dozen—the things I strive to do every day to live out my values and purpose. Let me share them with you:

1. Just for today … I will choose and display the right attitude.
2. Just for today … I will determine and act on important priorities.
3. Just for today … I will know and follow healthy guidelines.
4. Just for today … I will communicate with and care for my family.
5. Just for today … I will practice and develop good thinking.
6. Just for today … I will make and keep proper commitments.

7. Just for today … I will earn and properly manage finances.
8. Just for today … I will deepen and live out my faith.
9. Just for today … I will initiate and invest in solid relationships.
10. Just for today … I will plan for and model generosity.
11. Just for today … I will embrace and practice good values.
12. Just for today … I will seek and experience improvements.

Each of these decisions not only represents a strong value to be lived but is also a way to stay the course in the face of success or failure. These choices help me to keep my eye on success when I experience daily failure. They help me to embrace failure—instead of being embarrassed by it—and keep going. I have acted on these decisions and practiced these disciplines every day because I was confident that one day I would see the compounding results of many days lived well. And I have seen that belief pay off.

3. Keeping Failure and Success Together Develops Emotional Strength

Keeping failure and success together not only presents a true picture of life and allows wins and losses to complement each other, but it also helps us develop emotional strength. Pioneering sportswriter Grantland Rice said, "Failure isn't so bad if it doesn't attack the heart. Success is all right if it doesn't go to the head."[24] In other words, if we can navigate both situations effectively, we become stronger emotionally. That also brings maturity. I like the way author and theologian J. I. Packer described this when he wrote:

> A moment of conscious triumph makes one feel that after this nothing will really matter; a moment of realized

> disaster makes one feel that this is the end of everything. But neither feeling is realistic, for neither event is really what it is felt to be. The circumstances of triumph will not last, and the moment of triumph will sooner or later give way to moments of disappointment, strain, frustration, and grief, while the circumstances of disaster will prove to have in them seeds of recovery and new hope. Life in the world under God's providence is like that; it always has been, and always will be. … The mature person, who is mentally and emotionally an adult as distinct from a child, knows this and does not forget it.[25]

"Failure isn't so bad if it doesn't attack the heart. Success is all right if it doesn't go to the head."

—Grantland Rice

Keeping failure and success together, allowing neither to take you off course, strengthens you mentally and emotionally. And having that mental and emotional strength will enable you to continue keeping failure and success together. It's a self-perpetuating cycle. Tom Morris described this as a kind of stability in his book *Plato's Lemonade Stand.* He said:

> Imagine life as a big wagon wheel. If we emotionally live on the outer rim, then as the wheel turns, we are spun around to extreme highs and lows in rapid and dizzying succession. But if we can learn to move close to the mid-point of the hub, we become much more centered. The wheel will spin, but we won't be so dramatically thrown by its motion.[26]

If failure and success are located at the outer rim of life, then putting them together at the center of the hub helps us to stay centered and strong in a tumultuous world. And neither makes us dizzy. They simply become part of everyday life.

I became aware of how much I keep success and failure together at the center of my life during a recent Q&A session. Someone asked, "What was your most recent failure?" I quickly responded that I believed I had experienced a major failure in the last month. Then I started to think about it so that I could give a concrete example. But I became embarrassed because I couldn't think of one. My mind went blank, and I started getting frustrated with myself. However, when I tried to think of a recent big success, I realized I couldn't think of one of those, either. I was certain I'd experienced one in the last month, but again, no examples came to mind.

That's when I realized I've kept success and failure together for so long that neither stands out. I no longer experience strong highs or lows from them. Whether I experience failure or success, I try to learn from it, apply what I learn, and move on.

If you've spent most of your life striving for success and avoiding failure, keeping them far apart in your heart and mind, it may take you some time to get used to keeping them together. You may need to develop skills and habits to help you keep them close. If that's true, then take some advice from author and speaker Og Mandino. Here's how he described the way he kept himself on track:

If I feel depressed I will sing.

If I feel sad I will laugh.

If I feel ill I will double my labor.

If I feel fear I will plunge ahead.

If I feel inferior I will wear new garments.

If I feel uncertain I will raise my voice.

If I feel poverty I will think of wealth to come.

If I feel incompetent I will remember past success.

If I feel insignificant I will remember my goals.

Today I will be master of my emotions.[27]

Notice he said that every time he *felt* a negative emotion, he would *act* in a positive way to counterbalance it. That's what you can do. And every time you feel a strong positive emotion, you can temper it with humility and by using your success to take *action* to help other people.

Failure and success are much alike. They are not one-time events. Neither is a place where you will someday arrive. They are not who you are. Nor are they permanent. They are merely moments that illustrate how you deal with life along the way. Yes, you win. And lose. You will make mistakes. And do things well. You should never conclude that you are a failure. Or a success. You are in process and will be until you breathe your last breath. Until then, keep success and failure together. Don't let either one of them take you off course. Follow your purpose, do your best, and keep moving forward. Do that, and you will get a return on every investment in your life.

DISCUSSION QUESTIONS

If you're reading this book with a group or as part of a mastermind, use the discussion questions to explore ideas, share insights and struggles, and grow together.

1. **Have you ever experienced a tough year or rough time where you had to keep reminding yourself about your successes so that you could get through it? If so, describe it. If not, how could you set yourself up to help yourself in that way in the future?**

2. **What is the greatest lesson you've ever learned from a failure? What is the greatest lesson you've ever learned from a success? What difference do you notice between your examples?**

3. **Do you tend to think of yourself as a failure or a success? What is wrong with either of those ways of thinking?**

4. **How do you respond to the following statements: "You will never be a success. You have never been a failure. You will always be a person who fails and succeeds"?**

5. **What barriers to our potential might be created by separating failure and success in our minds? How does keeping success and failure together put people in a better position for the future?**

6. **How much of your energy do you expend trying to avoid failing? How much energy striving to be a success? How could that energy be put to better use to improve your life?**

7. **If you were to treat both failure and success as "imposters" and embrace the idea of traveling the road between, what criteria would you use to rate your progress?**

ACTION STEPS TO
KEEP SUCCESS AND FAILURE TOGETHER

Take these steps from the chapter to get a bigger return on failure in your life:

1. Find the Benefits of Keeping Success and Failure Together

Some of the benefits of keeping success and failure together were mentioned in the chapter: humility, resilience, and maturity to name three. Create your own list of positive benefits you will receive by keeping them together. For each benefit, describe how it will improve your life and increase your potential.

2. Stay Out of the Gutters

If you imagine failure and success as the gutters on either side of a road, most people avoid the failure gutter. But they don't realize they should also avoid the success gutter (because it can make us overconfident, unappreciative, and inattentive to asking good questions). Write a list of actions you can take to keep yourself emotionally out of the gutters and in the middle of the road where true life takes place.

3. Use Failure to Teach Your Greatest Lessons to Others

One of the best ways to appreciate failure and keep it together with success is to find the lesson in a failure and use it to teach others so they benefit from it. Consider the failure that has taught you life's greatest lesson so far. Spend time examining the failure, finding the lesson, breaking the experience down so you can teach it, and then communicate it to an audience who would welcome the teaching and benefit from it.

4. Give Reviewing Success and Failure Equal Weight

One of the best ways to bring success and failure together is to change how you review your successes. Create formal reviews for both. Design a process you can use for both. And give as much time to examining success as you do to failure.

3

To Get Over Failure, Get Over Yourself

Why is it so difficult for most people to deal with failure? Why does it get them down and stop them from accomplishing their best? It has been my observation that failure often becomes exaggerated and prolonged in people's lives because it feels so personal. And this is only made worse by our natural human tendency to be selfish and preoccupied with ourselves. In other words, we can't get over our failure because we can't get over ourselves.

ALL OF US MUST LEARN THIS LESSON

Poet James Russell Lowell observed, "No man can produce great things who is not thoroughly sincere in dealing with himself."[28] If we're honest, most of us will admit that we are more selfish than we want to be, and we must work hard to fight against it. That's the battle we must win if we want to develop maturity. But not everyone acknowledges their problem with self-centeredness. Recently, I was having a discussion with a lady, and in the course of the conversation, she said, "I have no selfishness in me."

Really? I thought. To anyone who thinks they've conquered their battle with self, I have one question: When you are shown a photograph taken of you in a group, what is the first thing you do? You look for *yourself*! We all do. Why? Because we are preoccupied with ourselves. If we look good in the picture, then we think it's a good picture, regardless of how others look. If we don't like the way we look, we want to take another picture.

If you've ever interacted with toddlers, you recognize that children are born selfish. Psychologist, professor, and author Burton L. White, who studied the dynamics of toddlers playing with one another, wrote what he called "The Toddler's Creed" to describe how small children interact with others:

> If I want it, it's mine.
>
> If I give it to you and change my mind later, it's mine.
>
> If I can take it away from you, it's mine.
>
> If I had it a little while ago, it's mine.
>
> If it's mine, it will never belong to anyone else, no matter what.
>
> If we are building something together, all the pieces are mine.
>
> If it looks like mine, it's mine.[29]

To overcome failure, each of us needs to conquer our inner toddler, getting over ourselves and looking beyond our selfish desires. When we can look beyond ourselves, we are better able to look beyond our failures.

What does it mean to get over yourself? It means

- Thinking beyond yourself,

- Loving beyond yourself,
- Serving beyond yourself,
- Giving beyond yourself, and
- Caring beyond yourself.

Note the repeated phrase. To develop the maturity and perspective to get over yourself, you need to get *beyond yourself.* One of the best ways to do this is to recognize the difference between success and significance. Success is mainly about helping ourselves. Significance is mainly about helping others. I hope you get to experience success in your life. I hope everyone does. But I hope even more that you experience significance because I know that without significance, success will leave your life unfulfilled. I know a lot of successful people who are unhappy. Only a life lived for others satisfies.

The person who taught me this most valuable lesson was my father, who lived a very significant life. He was my model and my inspiration. Two days before he passed away, I sat by his bedside for four hours and thanked him for all the lessons he taught me. I counted them and found that there were twenty-nine specific significant principles I learned from him. Later, as I reflected on those lessons, I realized nine of the twenty-nine were about other people:

Recognize the difference between success and significance. Success is mainly about helping ourselves. Significance is mainly about helping others.

- Add value to people.
- Encourage others.
- Walk slowly through the crowd.

- Live a generous life.
- Love people.
- See the best in others.
- Remember people's names.
- Travel the high road.
- Express gratitude to others.

Together, those lessons had an important message for me: "John, get over yourself!"

HOW TO GET OVER YOURSELF

One of the best things you can do for yourself—and others—is to get over yourself. You can do that by teaching yourself to think differently and to talk to yourself differently. Speaker and author Brian Tracy said, "Ninety-five percent of emotions are determined by the way you talk to yourself as you go throughout your day."[30] When we're selfish and self-centered, we tend to evaluate everything that happens to us by how it affects us, not by how it affects others. We take everything personally. When we do that, we can't help but be discouraged.

Trying to grow up and take things less personally is easy to say but hard to do. But I have some good news for you. There are specific steps you can take to become less preoccupied with yourself, get over yourself, and stop taking failure so personally. Here are seven steps you can take beginning today:

1. Stop Worrying About What Others Think of You

If we want to have a more contented life, we need to stop worrying so much about what others think of us. There's an old saying: "When you're twenty, you care what everyone thinks. When you're forty, you stop caring what everyone thinks. When you're sixty, you realize no one was ever thinking about you in the first place."[31] There's certainly a lot of truth in that. People think much less about us than we believe. And the opinions of strangers should mean very little to us. If we act in ways that value everyone, we don't need to worry about what people think because we know that we treat others well. And if the people closest to us love and respect us the most, then we can be certain we are on track. The less we worry about how others think of us, the more powerful we become.

Author and speaker Ernie Zelinski wrote:

> Participants in my seminars cite "the fear of failure" as a creative barrier or bandit; however, I point out to them that it isn't the fear of failure so much as the fear of what others will think about us. Many of us avoid taking risks because of our fear of looking bad if we fail. We get so obsessed with being liked that we won't do things which we feel may make us look bad in the eyes of others.[32]

Worrying too much about what others think can tie a person into all kinds of knots.

One evening, I was having dinner with my friends Brad and Julie Duncan. I asked them, "What is the best advice that you ever received?" I'll never forget Julie's answer: "My father said, 'Don't care so much about what other people think that it keeps you from living your best life.'" I wrote that down so that I could reflect on it. Later that night, I made that advice my own by phrasing it this way: Hold the perspective of others in proper perspective.

As I encourage you to stop worrying about what others think of you, does that mean you should ignore others' advice? Of course not.

We severely limit our growth if we refuse to listen to positive criticism from others. But we should consider the source when listening to opinions. I do that by taking into account the critic's perspective of me:

Questions to Ask About People's Perspectives

- *Do they care about me?*
- *Do they want what's best for me?*
- *Do they understand me?*
- *Do they want to help me or control me?*
- *Are they mature or self-centered?*

If someone is close to you and has your best interests at heart, then listen and learn. If not, don't worry so much about what they say, and don't take it personally. Take to heart the words of Hall of Fame baseball player Lou Brock, who said, "Show me a guy who's afraid to look bad, and I'll show you a guy you can beat every time."[33] If you want to become stronger emotionally and be able to withstand failure with grace and energy, stop taking what others say about you personally.

2. Put Some Distance Between Failure and Fault

One of the side effects of being too self-focused is assigning blame to ourselves when we fail. Too many people feel at fault when they fail, and they accuse themselves of being bad, stupid, careless, or valueless. While evaluating failure with the purpose of learning from it and improving ourselves is good, weighing ourselves down with fault and blame is not.

Harvard Business School professor Amy C. Edmondson studied the impact of failure on people and organizations. She wrote, "Failure and fault are virtually inseparable in most households, organizations, and cultures. Every child learns at some point that admitting failure means taking the blame."[34] This has a negative impact on performance because people want to avoid blame. She explained using the praiseworthy–blameworthy spectrum I mentioned in chapter 1:

> When I ask executives to consider this spectrum [of good and bad reasons for failure] and then to estimate how many of the failures in their organizations are truly blameworthy, their answers are usually in single digits—perhaps 2%–5%. But when asked how many are *treated* as blameworthy, they say (after a pause or a laugh) 70% to 90%. The unfortunate consequence is that many failures go unreported, and their lessons are lost.[35]

There is great value in separating fault from failure. Refusing to place blame on ourselves or others not only reduces the emotional toll failure takes on us; it also opens our minds to learning the lessons failure offers. If we frame failure more positively, without assigning fault, we take it less personally, and we become more open to its benefits. Corporate trainers and authors Joseph Grenny, Kerry Patterson, David Maxfield, Ron McMillan, and Al Switzler wrote about the importance of this, especially for people who tend to think about themselves negatively. They said:

This capacity to tell ourselves the right story about problems and setbacks is particularly important if we're already betting against ourselves. When faced with a setback, we need to learn to say "Aha! I've just discovered what doesn't work," and not, "Oh no! Once again, I'm an utter failure." We need to interpret setbacks as guides, not brakes.

Initially, failure signals the need for greater effort or persistence. Sometimes failure signals the need to change strategies or tactics. But failure should rarely signal that we'll never be able to succeed.[36]

If you're finding fault in yourself and taking failure personally, you're holding yourself back. It's time to put distance between failure and fault.

3. Become Comfortable with Rejection

In an old *Peanuts* comic strip, Charlie Brown complains to Linus about being rejected. "The publisher sent me a rejection slip," laments Charlie.

"So what," says Linus, "Lots of writers get rejection slips."

Charlie Brown cries out, "But I didn't even submit a manuscript."[37]

Contrast that story with this one about a real-life person's experience with rejection. Sometime in 1912, a young farmer, teacher, and aspiring writer from New England submitted poems to the editor of *The Atlantic Monthly*. The aspiring writer had managed to get a few poems published prior to this submission, but he was disappointed when he received a rejection from the highly regarded literary magazine's editor, Ellery Sedgwick, who wrote, "We are sorry that we have no place in *The Atlantic Monthly* for your vigorous verse."

That year, the writer moved with his family to England, but he didn't allow rejection to stop him from writing. During the next two years, while working on his small farm, he wrote more poetry and got two volumes of his work published in the United Kingdom to positive reviews. One critic lauded him as "a new American voice" in poetry. The books were *A Boy's Will* and *North of Boston*; the poet's name was Robert Frost.

In 1915, Frost returned home, and one of his poetry volumes was published in the United States. It was highly acclaimed, and he was instantly in demand as a speaker. He soon met Ellery Sedgwick in person at the offices of *The Atlantic Monthly*. The editor, who had previously rejected his work, offered to buy new poems from Frost sight unseen.[38]

Frost went on to publish numerous books of verse; be awarded three Pulitzer Prizes; receive teaching posts at Harvard, Dartmouth, and Amherst College; and serve as poetry consultant to the Library of Congress—the equivalent of being named the nation's poet laureate.[39] If Frost had taken rejection to heart and let it stop him from writing, he would have died an unknown farmer. Instead, he rejected rejection and fulfilled his purpose.

Financial expert and author Jeff Rose said, "The sooner you stop fearing rejection, the sooner you can become unstoppable." He wrote:

> Every successful entrepreneur or person has been through a laundry list of failures. As much as we love to glamorize risk-takers, we can't ignore how much they've failed on the road to success. One could even argue that the road to success is paved with failures and crushed dreams.
>
> The good news is every rejection or failure brings you one step closer to a yes that could change your entire life. They say that when one door closes, another one opens. This may not seem like the case at the moment, but those rejections will help you become more tenacious so that you're ready for whatever life throws at you.[40]

"The sooner you stop fearing rejection, the sooner you can become unstoppable."

—JEFF ROSE

No matter your history, profession, purpose, or aspirations, you will benefit from learning to reject rejection. It's simply another way of getting over yourself and working your way beyond failure to attain real achievement. As early movie star Mary Pickford said, "If you have made mistakes, even serious mistakes, there is always another chance for you. And supposing you have tried and failed again and again, you may have a fresh start any moment you choose, for this thing that we call 'failure' is not the falling down, but the staying down."[41] When you get knocked down, never feel sorry for yourself and stay down. Reject rejection, and get back up.

4. Follow the Twenty-Four-Hour Rule

My friend Ken Blanchard coauthored several books with Hall of Fame coach Don Shula, who won more games than any other National Football League (NFL) coach, led the Miami Dolphins to two Super Bowl victories, and coached Miami to the league's only perfect season in its history. Ken, who knew Don pretty well, wrote:

> Success is not forever and failure isn't fatal. This was Don Shula's favorite quote when he was the head coach of the Miami Dolphins. It drove a great deal of his behavior during his long and distinguished career as the winningest coach in the history of the NFL.
>
> Don had a twenty-four-hour rule. He allowed himself, his coaches, and his players a maximum of twenty-four hours after a football game to celebrate a victory or bemoan a defeat. During that time, they were encouraged to experience the thrill of victory or the agony of defeat as deeply as possible. Once the twenty-four-hour deadline had passed, they put it behind them and focused their energies on preparing for the next opponent. This is a principle well worth noting.

> Don't get a big head when you win or get too down in the dumps when you lose. Keep things in perspective. Success is not forever and failure is not fatal.[42]

I can't think of a better way to handle failure—or success. Give yourself twenty-four hours to experience and process it, and then move on. As someone pointed out, "You don't drown by falling into the water. You drown by staying there." Practicing the twenty-four-hour rule gets you out of deep water. It also allows you to simply turn your back on yesterday so you can embrace today. And trust me: If you want to be successful, today matters. It is the only day in which you can actually get anything done.

You don't drown by falling into the water. You drown by staying there.

5. Value Progress Over Perfection

We often miss opportunities because of our fear of failure. But the biggest failure is the failure to start, which is often caused by perfectionism. So many of us want to know everything up front before taking action. In an ideal world, that would be wonderful. In the real world, that is impossible. To be successful, we must take action first, then figure it out as we go.

Ryan Holiday, who wrote *The Obstacle Is the Way*, described what happens to us when we allow perfectionism to rule our lives and stop our progress:

> We often assume that the world moves at our leisure. We delay when we should initiate. We jog when we should be running or, better yet, sprinting. And then we're shocked—*shocked!*—when nothing big ever happens, when opportuni-

> ties never show up, when new obstacles begin to pile up, or the enemies finally get their act together.[43]

Instead of waiting for the perfect conditions to start, focus on progress over perfection. Your future self will thank you for the risks you take today. Psychologist Henry C. Link wrote, "While one person hesitates because he feels inferior, the other is busy making mistakes and becoming superior."[44] Striving for progress instead of perfection moves us forward *and* makes us better. But it requires us to take risks. That can be challenging and scary, but it gives us advantages:

The Advantages of Risk-Taking

- *We learn things faster than people who don't take risks.*
- *We have a broader and more mature range of experiences than those who don't take risks.*
- *We bump into obstacles sooner than people who don't take risks.*
- *We learn to overcome those obstacles that others don't.*

One of the best ways to convince ourselves to take steps forward in the face of uncertainty is to recognize that we cannot know all the answers before we move forward. Sometimes we have to follow our instincts, and only after we've taken many steps can we look back and see the pattern, the progress, and the place our path has led. In his commencement address at Stanford University in 2005, Steve Jobs explained this:

> You can't connect the dots looking forward; you can only connect them looking backward. So you have to trust that the dots will somehow connect in your future. You have to trust in something—your gut, destiny, life, karma, whatever. This approach has never let me down, and it has made all the difference in my life.[45]

If you believe you must line up the dots of your future and see everything in place before you move, you won't move. Instead, trust yourself, move forward, and take the dream journey. Years later, you will be able to look back on your life and connect the dots. And you will be amazed at what you accomplished because you didn't allow perfection to hold you back.

6. Become Too Big to Let Little Things Bother You

Winston Churchill said, "You will never reach your destination if you stop and throw stones at every dog that barks."[46] What a wonderful way of expressing the idea that we should not let little things bother us.

What's the best way to ensure that small things don't bother you? To become bigger yourself. By that I mean aspiring to achieve more significant things, striving to help more people, continuing to reach for higher goals, and learning and growing into your better self. At first, that can be hard because whenever we try to break new ground, we often fail. We are never good at anything the first time. That's certainly been true in my life. I played basketball during my growing-up years, but the first time I shot the ball, I missed the entire backboard. The first time I preached a sermon, it was a disaster. The first church I led in my career fell apart after I left. The first employee I hired and trained, I had to fire. Do I need to go on?

If you want to achieve anything worthwhile in life, you have to let go of what didn't work. You must have a short memory. You must keep improving. Here's how author and businessperson Glenn Van Ekeren put it:

> Successful people forget. They know the past is irrevocable. They're running a race. They can't afford to look behind.

> Their eye is on the finish line. Magnanimous people forget. They're too big to let little things disturb them. They forget easily. If anyone does them wrong, they consider the source and keep cool. It's only the small people who cherish revenge. Be a good forgetter. Business dictates it, and success demands it.[47]

If you see failure as a small thing, it will become small. The bigger you become as a person, the smaller and less significant your mistakes will feel. Author H. Stanley Judd said, "Don't waste energy trying to cover up failure. Learn from your failures and go on to the next challenge. It's OK to fail. If you're not failing, you're not growing."[48]

7. Focus on the Big Picture Instead of Yourself

In my book *Winning with People*, I teach The Big Picture Principle, which says that the entire population of the world, with one minor exception, is composed of others. In other words, I'm a minor exception. So are you. Everyone else in the world is more important than any one person. Therefore, it's essential that we always look beyond ourselves. We need to focus on the big picture of making the world a better place by helping others. We can do that if we choose to. In her classic book *To Kill a Mockingbird*, Harper Lee put these words in the judge's mouth during the dramatic courtroom scene: "People generally see what they look for and hear what they listen for."[49] That is a fact. Whatever you look for becomes your focus, and whatever you focus on becomes larger in your mind. If you look for the good, you'll find it. If you focus on the big picture, your perspective will improve. If you see others as more important than you, then your focus will be on *their* success, not *your* failure.

One of the leaders I greatly admire is former prime minister of the United Kingdom Winston Churchill. He did great things, but he also failed a lot. And through it all, he maintained the right perspective of himself. At a press conference, Churchill was asked by a reporter if he was thrilled by the crowds who attended his speeches. Churchill's reply showed that he saw a bigger picture: "It is quite flattering, but whenever I feel this way, I always remember that if instead of making a political speech I was being hanged, the crowd would be twice as big."[50]

Nobody makes all the right choices. Nobody avoids failure. Nobody lives a perfect life. To paraphrase author James M. Barrie, our lives are a diary in which we mean to write one story but write another, and our humblest hour is when we compare the two volumes. Most people desire success. Many people hope for greatness. All of us get stuck with our humanity. The question is, will we get over it? Will we get over ourselves?

I love something North Carolina basketball coach Dean Smith said: "If you make every game a life-and-death proposition, you're going to have problems. For one thing, you'll be dead a lot!"[51] I choose to live! With my humanity. With my shortcomings. With my failures. Since I can't choose to avoid them, I choose to get over them. I hope you will do the same.

"If you make every game a life-and-death proposition, you're going to have problems. For one thing, you'll be dead a lot!"

—DEAN SMITH

DISCUSSION QUESTIONS

If you're reading this book with a group or as part of a mastermind, use the discussion questions to explore ideas, share insights and struggles, and grow together.

1. **How did peer pressure affect you when you were a teenager? Did you ever do something because of peer pressure that you now find funny or embarrassing? If so, describe it.**

2. **What do you think of the statement of the woman who said, "I have no selfishness in me?" How would you rate your own level of selfishness on a scale of 1 to 10 with 10 being 100 percent selfish? How do you combat your natural selfishness?**

3. **Look at the questions to ask about people's perspective in the chapter. In the past, how often have you used questions like these to "consider the source" when you've been criticized? How might these questions help you in the future?**

4. **Has there been a time in your life when you experienced a major rejection, yet it did not negatively affect you or set you back? Why were you able to weather it so effectively?**

5. **The chapter suggested valuing progress over perfectionism. On a spectrum where excellence and perfectionism were on one end and progress and sloppiness were on the other, which side would you be on? (You're not allowed to say you're exactly in the middle.) How does your natural tendency help you? How does it work against you?**

6. **Based on the explanation of the big picture in the chapter, what would you say is the big picture for your life? How focused are you on it?**

7. **In your life, where do you most need to "get over yourself?" How do you need to change?**

ACTION STEPS TO
GET OVER FAILURE BY GETTING OVER YOURSELF

Take these steps from the chapter to get a bigger return on failure in your life:

1. Change Your Self-Talk

You may not talk to yourself out loud, but you have a commentary running in your head all day long. How do you talk to yourself? If that voice isn't positive and grace-giving, you need to change the way you talk to yourself. Starting tomorrow morning when you get up, pay attention to what you say to and about yourself, as well as the tone you use. If your thoughts are negative or your tone is critical or scolding, vow to change it. Give yourself the benefit of the doubt, and make an effort to be positive and encouraging.

2. Practice the Twenty-Four-Hour Rule

This week, choose to follow Don Shula's twenty-four-hour rule. When you experience a success or win at something, celebrate. Give yourself and others credit. But once twenty-four hours have passed, move on and don't think about it. Likewise, if you fail, make a mistake, or lose, give yourself twenty-four hours to be angry or grieve, and work to learn whatever lesson you can from the experience. But after twenty-four hours, stop thinking or talking about it.

3. Focus Your Attention Beyond Yourself

The best way to get over yourself is to start thinking beyond yourself. For the next two weeks, start each day by planning how you can help others. Think about how you can add value to others, love them, serve them, give to them, and care for them in the coming day. Schedule your intended actions, and then follow through. Take note of how moving your focus from self to others helps you to more positively deal with failure.

4. Work to Become Bigger

What are you doing to help yourself become bigger? Put yourself on a personal growth program that will help you to learn in your areas of strength, expand your thinking, increase your goals, and raise your level of performance. The work you do to grow must be daily or at least weekly, and should last at least six months but ideally a year or longer.

4

Use Failure to Make Yourself Better

Have you ever considered that failing might be exactly what you *need* to do so that you are able to do what you were always *meant* to do? That was the case for John James Audubon. Today we consider him one of the greatest wildlife artists of all time. His *Birds of America* is considered not only a meticulously accurate record of wildlife but also a beautiful work of art. An original copy of the book recently sold for $11.5 million.[52] But Audubon would never have created his masterpiece had he not failed.

As a young man of eighteen, Audubon was sent from France to America by his father to run a farm near Philadelphia. Through mismanagement, he lost the property. He tried working in banking at a counting house. Then started a retail business with a partner in Kentucky and later in Missouri. After several years of struggle, he gave that up and moved to New Orleans to start an import business.

Have you ever considered that failing might be exactly what you *need* to do so that you are able to do what you were always *meant* to do?

When that failed, he opened a mill, which also failed. At age thirty-four, he was bankrupt and was jailed for being in debt.[53]

This crushing failure opened the door for what he called his "great idea." The constants throughout Audubon's years of struggle were his hobbies of hunting, drawing, and painting. As he traveled, he always studied and sketched a wide variety of animals. Since all his other efforts had failed, he decided to dedicate himself to creating paintings of birds worthy of being bound into a great work. When he had created a large enough collection, he took his work to England, where the skills he'd learned in business helped him secure support, an engraver, and a printer. In the end, Audubon had his failure to thank for his success.

HOW FAILURE CAN MAKE YOU BETTER

Dale Carnegie said, "The successful man will profit from his mistakes and try again in a different way."[54] That's what John James Audubon did. For that matter, it's what Carnegie did. He experienced a long string of failures before finally writing *How to Win Friends and Influence People*, a perennial bestseller that has sold more than thirty million copies.[55]

"The successful man will profit from his mistakes and try again in a different way."

—Dale Carnegie

The truth is that you can *let* failure beat you down, or you can *use* failure to make yourself better. The choice is yours. If you're open to what failure can do for you, here are the ways you can use failure to improve yourself and your situation:

1. Failure Can Make You More Resilient

Bouncing back from failure is one of the most valuable abilities a human being can possess. Unfortunately, it's a skill that many people today have a difficult time developing. Perhaps that's because modern medicine, technology, and innovation have improved our quality of life. If you look back a century, you can see that people bounced back from adversity because they faced so much of it.

A good example of this was Thomas Edison, who could be dubbed Mr. Resilient. His ability to try, fail, and try again was legendary. The company's failures outnumbered its successes to such a degree that it's astounding he never quit. For example, in his quest to find a native plant-based source for rubber, his lab failed in tens of thousands of attempts to identify a viable source. It's said a discouraged assistant complained, "Mr. Edison, we have made fifty thousand experiments and have had no results."

"Results!" exclaimed the inventor with enthusiasm. "We have wonderful results. We now know fifty thousand things which won't work!"[56]

Edison didn't even give up when most of his laboratory burned down. After watching the fire, which was so huge that it drew six to eight whole fire *departments*, Edison said, "Although I am over sixty-seven years old, I'll start all over again tomorrow." And he did. He began rebuilding the next morning![57]

How can you become more resilient as you deal with failure? Start by cultivating these practices:

- **Self-Compassion**: Show kindness toward yourself and others involved in the failure. Focus on empathy and keeping the failure in perspective. Admitting failure is positive. Beating yourself up over it is not.

- **Recognition:** It's beneficial to appreciate the efforts that you and others have made in the effort to succeed—even when you don't achieve your goal. Value the process as much as or more than the outcome to frame your thinking with a more positive outlook.
- **Active Learning:** By default, we respond defensively or cast blame when we fail. Instead, take a learner's approach. Rather than being judgmental, take time to reflect and understand what went wrong, what to change, and how to be different going forward.
- **Cognitive Agility:** If you can acknowledge your part in failure, process your emotions quickly, and learn from it, you will be able to pivot to new opportunities. This is a major difference-maker and a sign of resilience.
- **Problem Solving:** If you can stay curious, creative, and open as you move forward to pursue new opportunities, you will be quicker at solving problems *before* you experience failure. Continue to collect data to inform your decisions and next steps.
- **Finding Meaning:** When you're done processing failure and learning from it, don't focus on regrets. Reconnect with the larger meaning behind the goal you missed, and use that to get back on your feet and keep trying.

For years I had a sign in my office that read, "Yesterday Ended Last Night." It was my reminder to be resilient, get back into the game, and keep moving forward, no matter what happened the day before. I want to encourage you not to get emotionally stuck when you fail, but to bounce back. Learn, improve, and get back in the game.

2. Failure Gives You a Reason to Reflect

Why do some people make the same mistakes over and over again? Because they never take the time to reflect. How can anyone discover *why* they made a mistake if they never examine their actions?

I'm fortunate because I experienced a significant failure in my career in my mid-twenties. It really shook me because I thought I'd been successful and didn't understand that I had actually failed until afterward. And it ate at me. I spent weeks thinking about it before I finally figured out what I'd done wrong, and I changed the way I led people to avoid making the same mistake again. That's how I discovered the value of reflection. That experience led me to develop a process for evaluating my experiences—both positive and negative—through reflection. Here's what I do:

Review by Myself

I have made it a regular practice in my life to review and reflect. Yes, I still take time to think about my major failures and successes, but I also take a moment every evening to assess my day and measure the contributions I made to others. I also examine how I need to improve.

Ask Questions of Myself

How do I direct my reflection? By asking myself questions. Every evening, I ask the following:

- What happened in my world today?
- What did I learn about myself today?
- Is there anything I need to make right?
- How can I do better tomorrow?
- What do I need to change?

This is where I really examine myself and learn.

Talk to Myself

Asking myself questions helps me to know what I think and feel about my actions as I reflect. To keep myself from becoming negative or feeling discouraged, I talk to myself in response. I work to keep my perspective positive, keeping in mind what I need to hear myself say. This is important. My friend Brian Tracy stated, "Psychologists say that fully 95 percent of your emotions are determined by the way you talk to yourself as you go through your day. … The sad fact is that if you do not deliberately and consciously talk to yourself in a positive and constructive way, you will, by default, think about things that will make you unhappy or cause you worry and anxiety."[58]

"Psychologists say that fully 95 percent of your emotions are determined by the way you talk to yourself as you go through your day."

—Brian Tracy

Direct Myself

At the end of my reflection time, I strive to deal with myself honestly. The most important part of that is taking appropriate action immediately. If I reflect but don't act, then I'm left with nothing but good intentions. What changes me and changes my world are good actions.

I encourage you to use failure to improve yourself through reflection. After every failure, review your actions and the outcome. Ask yourself difficult questions and answer them honestly. Look for ways to improve, coach yourself to remain positive, and then take action. You will be astounded by how much this helps you.

3. Failure Can Help You Develop Good Character

Professor and author Brené Brown said, "What we know matters, but who we are matters more."[59] What she's describing is character, which is the core and foundation of every person. Developing character is a never-ending process, and our response to failure is a major determining factor for who we are. The stronger we are in the face of defeat, holding onto our core values, the better our character becomes.

"What we know matters, but who we are matters more."

—Brené Brown

I remember well a life-changing conversation I had with the CEO of a very successful company. As we talked, I admired his honesty and openness about his past failures in leadership. His authenticity prompted me to ask if he could ever go back to some of his biggest failures and whether he would want the chance to have any do-overs.

"No," he replied. "My failures have helped me do two things: learn from them and develop character because of them. If I did a do-over, I'd lose many of my most important life lessons. And I wouldn't be the person I am today." He is a perfect example of someone who understands how to get a return on failure.

If you can face the hardships of life while retaining your values and bouncing back, you can come back much stronger than you were before. Your losses will become lessons that strengthen you from the inside out. And you will be able to tackle bigger and more difficult challenges in your life. You'll be able to live out an observation made by Indian activist leader Mahatma Gandhi, who said, "A [person] of character will make himself worthy of any position he is given."[60]

4. Failure Can Deepen Your Humility

One of the greatest obstacles to learning and improvement is pride. It makes us think, *I already learned that*. In contrast, humility tells us, *I need to learn more*. And when we're open to learning, especially in the face of failure, we can become better.

Humility and a learner's mindset are like the chicken and the egg. Which comes first? It's hard to say. If you're not sure or if you have a problem with pride, then embrace the mindset of a learner to start the humility cycle. That's what I have tried to do. And here's how it has shaped me:

- I learned people skills by dealing with difficult people.
- I learned to listen when a good friend told me I didn't do that.
- I learned leadership when I realized others weren't following me.
- I learned about forgiveness when I realized I needed someone to forgive me.
- I learned to ask questions when I ran out of answers.
- I learned not to take myself seriously when I understood that no one else did.
- I learned to take better care of myself after I experienced a heart attack.

Humility is one of the greatest virtues. It protects you. As Mother Teresa said, "If you are humble nothing will touch you, neither praise nor disgrace, because you know what you are."[61] Develop humility and keep learning in response to failure, and you will become a better person.

"If you are humble nothing will touch you, neither praise nor disgrace, because you know what you are."

—Mother Teresa

---

5. Failure Can Help You Gain Wisdom

Most of the wisdom we can acquire in life comes from failure. I love the way Oprah Winfrey expressed this in a commencement speech. She challenged the graduates:

> Turn your wounds into wisdom. You will be wounded many times in your life. You'll make mistakes. Some people will call them *failures* but I have learned that failure is really God's way of saying, "Excuse me, you're moving in the wrong direction." It's just an experience, just an experience.[62]

Wisdom can come to us when we recognize the difference between what we cannot control and what we can, when we realize that some things we can understand and some things we can't. Knowing which is which requires thoughtfulness and life experience. A mindset of wisdom is expressed in the Serenity Prayer, originally written by Reinhold Niebuhr and later adapted by Alcoholics Anonymous: "God, give us grace to accept with serenity the things that cannot be changed, courage to change the things that should be changed, and the wisdom to distinguish the one from the other."[63]

In life, we often discover what we *can* do by finding out what we *cannot* do. If we don't allow where we fall short to defeat us, we gain wisdom. We need to remember that failure is a temporary result of the actions we've taken that didn't work out. On the other hand, defeat is a choice we make.

Failure is a temporary result of the actions we've taken that didn't work out. On the other hand, defeat is a choice we make.

6. Failure Observed Can Give You Insight

One of the smartest and least painful ways to learn from failure is to gain insight from observing others who have failed. I mentioned in chapter 2 that I often schedule learning lunches where I interview someone I admire and want to learn from. One question I always ask is, "How has failure shaped your life?" I can't begin to tell you how many lessons I've learned and insights I've gained from hearing others' stories of failure and what they learned from them. Here are just a few insights I picked up by observing and listening:

- Cut your losses quickly.
- Think of your problems as challenges.
- A loss is better than a cheap win.
- Give 60 percent, and take 40 when making a deal.
- All is well that begins well.
- Leaders need to become self-aware and situationally aware.
- Live by principle, not by pressure.
- People see what they expect to see.
- Take pride in your choices, not your gifts.
- Understand the value of necessary endings.

If you're a stubborn or prideful person, you may be resistant to asking for advice or allowing others to instruct you. If that's you, then you might want to heed the lesson in a story called "The Rude Parrot":

> A young man named John received a parrot as a gift. The parrot had a bad attitude and an even worse vocabulary. Every word out of the bird's mouth was rude, obnoxious and laced with profanity.

John tried and tried to change the bird's attitude by consistently saying only polite words, playing soft music and anything else he could think of to "clean up" the bird's vocabulary.

Finally, John was fed up and he yelled at the parrot. The parrot yelled back. John shook the parrot and the parrot got angrier and even ruder.

John, in desperation, threw up his hands, grabbed the bird and put him in the freezer. For a few minutes the parrot squawked and kicked and screamed. Then suddenly there was total quiet. Not a peep was heard for over a minute.

Fearing that he'd hurt the parrot, John quickly opened the door to the freezer. The parrot calmly stepped out onto John's outstretched arms and said, "I believe I may have offended you with my rude language and actions. I'm sincerely remorseful for my inappropriate transgressions and I fully intend to do everything I can to correct my rude and unforgivable behavior."

John was stunned at the change in the bird's attitude. As he was about to ask the parrot what had made such a dramatic change in his behavior, the bird continued, "May I ask what the turkey did?"[64]

Even the most stubborn person can become teachable and learn from the mistakes of others.

7. Failure Can Prompt You to Ask Good Questions

I've touched on the importance of asking questions a few times in this book, so you're probably starting to understand how crucial I believe they are, not only for receiving a return on failure but also for personal growth and successful leadership. As you learn to use failure to improve yourself, you should make it your goal to shift from questioning whether you're a failure to asking good questions about each failure you experience.

The more I've used questions to examine failure, the better and faster I've become at processing failure, learning from it, making adjustments, and moving forward. And that's been especially important as I've taken on greater and more difficult leadership tasks. The higher you go, the more often you need to make decisions based on limited or unclear information.

Author and business leader Jay Coughlan, who believes he has failed more often than most entrepreneurs, says that every time he or his team experienced a failure, he would lead them through a debriefing session that consisted of three questions:

1. **What did I (or we) do right?** In this situation, most people start off by asking what they did wrong. This question puts many on the defensive. Anyway, in most cases you're doing something right. Start with "What did I (we) do right?" because it helps change your paradigm, which helps you build on what's presently working.
2. **In hindsight, what would I (or we) have done differently?** This question increases your prudence in decision-making. Now that you have more information, question how you would apply this wisdom for a better outcome the next time. This valuable process will help you improve and grow from mistakes.
3. **What am I (or we) going to change?** You might have seven things you would do differently but have the ability to change

> only one or two of them in the next month. Stay focused on the most important changes you need to make and then come back and do this debriefing exercise in another month. Asking this question helps you better adapt to necessary change.[65]

I like Coughlan's approach because it is positive and focused, and the goal is incremental, positive improvement. Asking yourself these kinds of questions is one of the best ways to use failure to make yourself better.

8. Failure Can Challenge You to Eliminate Excuses

I remember a *Peanuts* comic strip by Charles Schulz where Linus, the statistician for their baseball team, goes to Charlie Brown to deliver a report. "I've compiled the statistics on our baseball team for last season," Linus says. "In twelve games, we almost scored a run. In nine games, the other team almost didn't score before the first out. In right field, Lucy almost caught three balls and once almost made the right play." Linus then concludes, "We led the league in 'almosts,' Charlie Brown."[66]

While I strongly recommend that we try to remain positive while looking at our failures, calling everything an "almost success" doesn't really do us any good. It has about the same value as making excuses. Why? Because it's self-deceptive. If we're making excuses, we'll never see where we went wrong or learn how to make improvements.

Excuses are exits off the road to success. Every time we fall short and explain it away by saying we didn't do it, couldn't do it, shouldn't do it, didn't think about it, or didn't try, we fall farther behind and farther away from where we want to go.

Excuses are not only deceptive; they can be habit-forming. They can keep us in a rut of failure. The more reasonable sounding the excuse, the worse it is for us because we buy into it. To eliminate excuses, we must be aware that we're making them. As my friend Chris Hodges says, "You can make excuses, or you can make progress, but you cannot make both."

"You can make excuses, or you can make progress, but you cannot make both."
—Chris Hodges

---

9. Failure Can Prompt You to Change

If you've spent more time in your life avoiding failure than using it to help you improve, then I have good news for you. You can change. One of my favorite sayings is this: "Though you cannot go back and make a brand-new start, my friend, anyone can start from now and make a brand-new end."[67]

It's been said that you can't teach an old dog new tricks. I'm not sure about that, but I do know that there is no age limit on learning from our failures. A favorite memory of my dad was watching him take notes at a lecture he attended—when he was ninety-four years old! He was still learning, changing, and growing until the day he died. I intend to do the same. I hope you do too!

Failure and mistakes can be hard on everyone. They can make people feel defeated. I think many people approach life like students who take a test, don't know the answers, and get a bad grade. But life isn't like school—at least, not the schools I attended. The point isn't to get a good grade the first time. It's to learn through the whole process so that you know more every day and are better prepared for whatever's next.

I love the way my friend Ken Blanchard approached teaching people and helping them learn when he taught at the University of San Diego. Author Gary Burnison wrote about Ken's method:

> He always gave out copies of the final exam on the first day of class so that students would know exactly what they were expected to learn. The rest of the course was devoted to helping students master the concepts and material. Ken's university colleagues, however, were up in arms. Why would he do such a thing as giving students the final exam from the beginning of the class? Ken explained his purpose—his "mission statement" of what he intended the outcome to be: "I don't want them to fail," Ken said. "I want them to learn."[68]

If you learn—no matter how difficult a time you have or how catastrophic a failure you experience—you will improve. You will become a better person, a better leader, and a better worker in your profession. And that's the key to success and contentment in life. Growth is a reward that makes every aspect of life better. And it prepares you to do bigger, better, and harder things, which is the subject of the next chapter.

DISCUSSION QUESTIONS

If you're reading this book with a group or as part of a mastermind, use the discussion questions to explore ideas, share insights and struggles, and grow together.

1. **In what way, if any, can you relate to the life of John Audubon? What lessons can you learn from his story?**

2. **How resilient do you consider yourself to be? How do you rate yourself on a scale from 1 to 10 with 10 representing the ability to bounce back from anything? Why do you give yourself that score? What role does resilience play in being able to use failure to make yourself better?**

3. **How have failures, mistakes, problems, and setbacks developed your character? Give an example of a value you identified after a negative experience.**

4. **What is your best learning style? Do you learn from reading, listening, watching, doing, or via some other method? Give an example of something you've learned using your best style.**

5. **How can you harness that style to help you learn and improve yourself after failing?**

6. **Was there ever a time in your life when you tended to make excuses instead of trying to learn when you fell short or made mistakes? How did you overcome excuse-making? If you haven't yet done that, what must you do to change?**

7. **What is your greatest obstacle to using failure to learn and make yourself better? What could you do to overcome that obstacle?**

ACTION STEPS TO USE FAILURE TO MAKE YOURSELF BETTER

Take these steps from the chapter to get a bigger return on failure in your life:

1. Develop the Humility Needed to Learn

We all need to examine whether pride is holding us back from learning, but it's difficult because we are often unable to see it in ourselves. To help you overcome this problem, ask several people you can trust to give you an honest opinion to score how prideful you are on a scale of 1 to 10, with 10 being the most prideful. If your average score is higher than a 3, develop a strategy to help you soften your pride so that you can become more humble and teachable.

2. Learn to Coach Yourself

Use the guidelines in the chapter to coach yourself by reviewing your week, asking yourself questions about how you can learn and change, talking to yourself to decide what actions you need to take, and directing yourself to follow through. Keep a log or journal recording each session. Repeat this process for four to six weeks and then look back to evaluate your progress.

3. Take Time to Reflect

Set aside time to write down the major life lessons you've learned from failure, mistakes, problems, and conflict. Reflect on those lessons. What can you learn about yourself from them? How can those insights help you deal with adversity in the future?

4. Connect Problems and Purpose

Have you ever considered that failing is what you *needed* to do to make it possible for you to do what you're *meant* to do? If you have a sense of what your purpose in life is, identify how past failures have given you skills or insight to pursue it. If you lack a sense of purpose, examine your past failures for insight or patterns that might help you understand what you are meant to do.

5

Embrace the Value of Hard

I started studying leadership with intensity in the early seventies, soon after I started my first job as a leader. Back then, management books were easy to find, but few books focused on leadership. I read everything I could find, observed the best leaders I knew, and studied history. After several years of observing leaders and leading people myself, I came to an important realization: Everything rises and falls on leadership. In any situation or organization, when the leadership is good, everything rises—the people, the organization, the mission, the achievements, and the momentum. And when leadership is bad, all those things fall.

I came to that conclusion in 1974, and soon afterward, it became my mission to teach leadership to others. To my astonishment, many of the people I wanted to help were disinterested in learning how to lead. The first time I held a leadership seminar, fewer than ten people signed up. Even though we charged a fee, we lost money because running the seminar cost more than the amount we brought in.

I didn't allow that to stop me from communicating the importance of leadership. I continued to host leadership seminars, but I was surprised by people's responses when I invited them to attend. "I'm already a leader. Why should I attend your seminar?" people often said. They thought that having a position or title meant that they were already leaders. They didn't understand that leading requires skill. Leadership can be learned, and when a leader gets better, so does everything for the people they lead.

To help people understand leadership and how influence works, I developed a lesson called The 5 Levels of Leadership. You may be familiar with it if you've read some of my other books. The essence of the idea is that leadership is based on influence, position is the lowest level of leadership, and leadership influence is based on our interactions with others as we help them and the team.

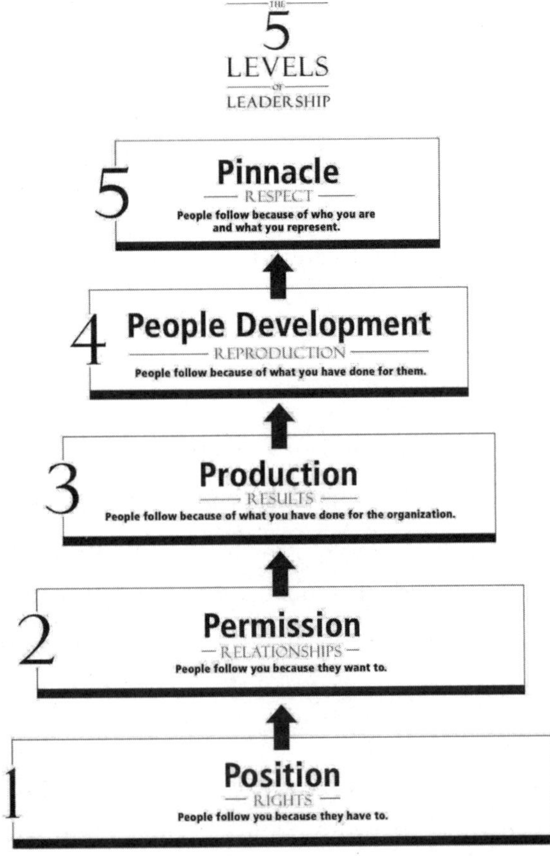

When people still resisted the idea of learning to improve their leadership ability, I grew frustrated. What does a person do when he keeps failing in what he considers to be one of his most important missions in life?

Around that same time, I read M. Scott Peck's book *The Road Less Traveled*. The opening paragraph of the first chapter changed my perspective:

> Life is difficult.
>
> This is a great truth, one of the greatest truths. It is a great truth because once we truly see this truth, we transcend it. Once we truly know that life is difficult—once we truly understand and accept it—then life is no longer difficult. Because once it is accepted, the fact that life is difficult no longer matters.[69]

That's when it occurred to me: Of course teaching leadership was hard. That's life. Hard is normal, and I needed to accept it.

"Once we truly know that life is difficult—once we truly understand and accept it—then life is no longer difficult."

—M. Scott Peck

CLIMB THE HILL

I embraced Peck's words. I memorized that passage from the book. I talked about his message and taught it to others. And I was determined to embrace it and benefit from it. Today, more than forty years later, I teach that same idea in my own words. Everything worthwhile is uphill. If you want to get anywhere in life, you will need to accept this truth. It's the only way you will be able to get a return on failure.

In life, you're either doing the hard work of climbing uphill, or you're allowing yourself to slide downhill. There really is no standing still. Gravity has a pull that will take us downward unless we resist it. Take a look at the differences between the two:

UPHILL CLIMBING	DOWNHILL SLIDING
Everything Worthwhile	**Nothing Worthwhile**
Wins	**Losses**
Preparing	**Repairing**
High Morale	**Low Morale**
Self-Respect	**Self-Regret**
Self-Improvement	**No Improvement**
Purposeful	**Aimless**
Fulfilling	**Empty**
Making a Difference	**Making No Difference**
Intentional Actions – Doing	**Good Intentions – Waiting**

If you want to achieve anything in life, you need to embrace the value of hard and accept that climbing is challenging, strenuous, difficult, and sometimes even grueling. You must be intentional, willful, and consistent to arrive anywhere worth going.

Do you want great relationships with others? Well, you're going to have to work at them because developing them is going to be hard. Do you want to grow to reach your maximum potential? You can't glide or slide there; it's going to be hard. Do you want to achieve success? Do you want to feel significant? Do you want to live a life that makes a difference? Me too. And yes, all those things are going to be hard. If you want to achieve all the things you desire in life, you must be willing to climb uphill. You need to embrace the value of hard.

In 2000, I took a group of leaders on a tour of Israel. One of our destinations was Masada, an ancient mountaintop fortress that was the site of a Roman siege in AD 72. Masada stands more than fourteen hundred feet above the desert floor not far from the Dead Sea. Most people ride to the summit on a gondola. But our group planned to hike to the top together. At the base of the mountain, we took this picture.

We knew it wasn't going to be easy, but we expected it to be an unforgettable experience. And it was. Our time at the top was that much sweeter because we had worked for it.

CHARACTERISTICS OF HARD

To continually receive a positive return on failure, you must embrace the value of hard. You will be able to do that only when you understand the *reality* of hard. To help you with that, I want to present six characteristics of hard that you would be wise to recognize, understand, and embrace:

1. Hard Never Ends

When I started my career, I understood nothing about success, failure, or the value of hard. I had destination disease. I believed I would work hard for a season, climb to the top of the mountain of success, and rest there without failures or problems. I couldn't have been more wrong! I think many of us underestimate the difficulties we will face in life as we try to achieve our goals.

Business leader Ernest Davenport gave a speech many years ago in which he told the story of a young baseball player who was invited to spring training by a professional team. Each week, the young player contacted his mother to report his progress. The first week, he said, "Dear Mom, leading all the batters. These pitchers are not so tough." A week later, he boasted, "Looks like I will be a starting infielder. Now hitting .500." But early in the third week, the young man's mother received a different kind of message. "Dear Mom," it said. "They started throwing curves. Will be home Friday."[70]

To increase your return on failure and to achieve lasting success, you can't pin all your hopes on a goal or a destination. Why? Because if you never reach it, you'll believe you're a failure, which won't be true. And if you do reach it, you won't keep growing and strive for anything else, which will *make* you a failure. Instead, you must learn to embrace the climb. And you must be determined to *keep* climbing.

Texas businessman Fred Smith, who was one of my mentors, encouraged me to stop thinking of success as a destination and instead focus on continuing to grow. Fred said:

> Something in human nature tempts us to stay where we're comfortable. We try to find a plateau, a resting place, where we have comfortable stress and adequate finances. Where we have comfortable associations with people, without the intimidation of meeting new people and entering strange situations.
>
> Of course, all of us need to plateau for a time. We climb and then plateau for assimilation. But once we've assimilated what we've learned, we climb again. It's unfortunate when we've done our last climb. When we have made our last climb, we are old, whether forty or eighty.[71]

"It's unfortunate when we've done our last climb. When we have made our last climb, we are old, whether forty or eighty."

—Fred Smith

When you acknowledge that everything worthwhile is uphill and you embrace the climb, you accept that you are in for the long haul. You know better than to expect immediate results. You apply your energy and time in measured increments and celebrate milestones of success along the way. This gives you staying power. That's what you need when you realize that hard never ends.

I once taught my staff a lesson called It's the Grind that Gets 'Em. I wrote it in response to a quote attributed to William Booth, founder of the Salvation Army: "If you want to really lead, you must be willing to grind." I believe life is a grindstone, and we have two choices when dealing with it. We can let it grind us down or polish us up. That's what I wanted to communicate to my staff.

Understanding that hard never ends helps us to stop expecting to be overnight successes. Instead, we embrace the idea of developing a lifetime of success. How?

We show up every day.
We do the work.
We embrace hard.
We try new things.
We fail.
We improve.
We grow.
We face countless challenges and rejections.
We doubt ourselves.
We want to quit.
But we don't.
We continue.
And we do it all over again.

If we do that, we will get a return on failure, and we will achieve more than we ever expected to achieve in our lives.

2. Hard Teaches Us That the Way Up Is Down

Several years ago, Richard Rohr wrote a book called *Falling Upward.* In it, he taught that the key to a fulfilling and genuinely successful life on a deeper level comes from experiencing our downs. He wrote:

> The soul has many secrets. They are only revealed to those who want them, and are never completely forced upon us. One of the best-kept secrets, and yet one hidden in plain sight, is that *the way up is the way down*. Or, if you prefer, *the way down is the way up*. This pattern is obvious in all of nature, from the very change of the seasons and substances on this earth, to the six hundred million tons of hydrogen that the sun burns every day to light and warm our earth. … The down-up pattern is constant, too, in mythology, in stories like that of Persephone, who must descend into the underworld and marry Hades for spring to be reborn.
>
> In legends and literature, sacrifice of something to achieve something else is almost the only pattern. Dr. Faust has to sell his soul to the devil to achieve power and knowledge; Sleeping Beauty must sleep for a hundred years before she can receive the prince's kiss. In Scripture, we see that the wrestling and wounding of Jacob are necessary for Jacob to become Israel (Genesis 32:26–32), and the death and resurrection of Jesus are necessary to create Christianity. The loss and renewal pattern is so constant and ubiquitous that it should hardly be called a secret at all. … The pattern in fact is so clear that one has to work rather hard, or be intellectually lazy, to miss the continual lesson.[72]

Loss can lead to gain if our attitudes toward failure are right. We must fall and learn from failure to be able to get up and move upward. Rohr called this "necessary suffering." It's necessary because we need it to make us stronger and thus better able to climb. But it's also necessary because as human beings, falling *will* happen to us.

The COVID-19 pandemic introduced new generations to inconvenience and suffering. Loss of life was the greatest tragedy many faced. But for everyone, the normal way of doing things was interrupted, and nothing seemed the same. That's a hardship. But it also offers a lesson. I thought of it as taking a detour. Since your life is being detoured, accept that journey and look for things you have never seen before. Learn new things you have not experienced. Maybe by traveling a "wrong way," you can find a better way. You can receive a return on failure if you accept this necessary suffering and allow it to make you a better person.

3. Hard Is About What You Do, Not What You Want

Wanting something is easy. *Doing* something is harder. Dreams are free, but the journey we must take and what we must pay to achieve them are not. What we do not only determines what we accomplish; it also determines who we become.

One of my favorite books is *Atomic Habits* by James Clear. He teaches that our behavior determines who we become. He wrote:

> The more you repeat a behavior, the more you reinforce the identity associated with that behavior. In fact, the word *identity* was originally derived from the Latin words *essentitas*, which means being, and *identidem*, which means repeatedly. Your identity is literally your "repeated beingness."[73]

You can make a shift in your identity by choosing to be a different person. How? By doing things different from the way you've done them before. But you must embrace hard to take those steps and become that improved person. Do you want to be a leader? Do what's hard: Lead. Do you want to be a writer? Do what's hard: Write. Do you want to be a better parent, spouse, sibling, or child? Do the hard work of acting like one. Do you want to be healthy? Do the hard work of eating right, sleeping well, and exercising. If you're willing to embrace hard, you can accomplish almost anything.

***Wanting* something is easy. *Doing* something is harder. Dreams are free, but the journey we must take and what we must pay to achieve them are not.**

4. Hard Is the Seed of Growth

Napoleon Hill said, "Every failure brings with it the seed of an equivalent success."[74] Why did he believe that? Because we learn more from failure than from success, and we can find a seed of growth in failure if we look for it. Adversity reveals the truth that the path of life is hard. It always has been and always will be.

"Every failure brings with it the seed of an equivalent success."
—Napoleon Hill

When I started my career, speaking was not easy for me. Nor was I successful. In the beginning, the crowds were small. And I was boring. (That's one of the reasons the crowds were small!) It took me ten years of failures and adjustments to learn how to become a communicator. It felt hard, but that decade of growth planted the seeds of success I experience today, allowing me to speak to millions of people every year.

Writing wasn't easy for me either. Putting thoughts on paper was laborious, and I simply wasn't able to make words come alive. And as a result, my books didn't sell well. However, by my fifth book, I started to turn the corner. And my eleventh book became a bestseller. Success showed up in book eleven. But the seeds of success were sown during the hard years of growth as I worked on the first ten books. My improvements had to be stored up before they showed up.

Several years ago, I read a poem called "Climb the Steep." It describes the challenges and benefits of adversity and how it can help us grow:

For every hill I've had to climb
For every rock that bruised my feet
For all the blood and sweat and grime
For blinding storms and burning heat
My heart sings but a grateful song
These were the things that made me strong
For all the heartaches and the tears
For all the misery and the pain
For the gray days and useless years
And for the hopes that lived in vain
I do give thanks for now I know
These were the things that helped me grow

It's not the softer things of life
That arouse our will to strive

> But, raw adversity and strife
> Do most to keep our will alive
> Over rose strewn paths the anointed ones creep
> But only those deserted dare climb the steep
>
> And are all the better for it............[75]

To fertilize the seed of growth during tough times, forget about your past achievements and allow yourself to become a beginner again. Have a learning mindset. And if you're a person of faith, ask the God who made you to keep remaking you.

5. Hard Values What You Have Been Through

The most important steps of growth we can take are always internal, and those most often come as the result of hardship. People who embrace their tough times and value what they learn have the strength to look reality in the eye and keep moving forward, even when they find it difficult.

Someone who has done this and has spent his life helping others do the same is John Hope Bryant, the founder, chairman, and CEO of Operation HOPE, a nonprofit organization that strives to help people who are underserved and lack opportunities. Not long ago, I had one of my learning lunches with him so that I could learn from him. I really like his perspective:

> Most people find strength in things that are outside them: money, power, titles, wardrobes, cars. But most of the things that make a leader are on the inside: integrity, wisdom, confidence, vulnerability, joy, passion, compassion, intuition. These things come from life experience, from life's trials,

from the deepest part of a person's soul. You can't fake them, and you can't buy what's not for sale.

My mentor Rev. Murray says, "Life asks a question of every leader that gauges their effectiveness and wisdom: 'What have you been through?'" Following battle King Arthur would have his knights line up before him, asking of each, "Show me your scars." If none existed, he would say to the warrior, "Leave me and go get your scars."

I have learned that authenticity counts, and that the best route to an authentic life is through your scars. As you earn them, you learn to drop the BS in your life and to attach yourself to the substance in your life—and to the substance in those around you. Precisely because of that history of loss, you never take yourself too seriously or get needlessly seduced by short-term materialism. In other words, loss helps ground you as a person.

There's a hard lesson in life's setbacks: *just as steel is forged through fire, leaders are forged through loss.* There can be no strength, no real inner growth, without the pain of legitimate suffering. It's a scientific fact: you cannot have a rainbow without a storm.[76]

"Life asks a question of every leader that gauges their effectiveness and wisdom: 'What have you been through?'"

—REV. MURRAY

Bryant believes that a lot of people don't strive to learn life lessons from hardship and failure because they find the process too difficult or painful. I agree with his assessment. It requires determination and intentionality, but successful people embrace that process. Because they value what hard teaches them, they don't shy away from it. And that learning opens the door to improvement and greater success.

6. Hard Gets Harder Unless You Change Your Perspective

I once read a funny story about a college student who decided to take his girlfriend home to meet his mom. His mother made it clear very quickly that she did not approve of his girlfriend, so when he got back to campus, he broke up with her. Later, when he started dating another young woman, he took her home, and Mom disdained her too. The young man started to wonder if it was impossible to please his mother, so he started inviting home one young woman after another just to see if he could please his mother—but to no avail. Finally, he found someone so like his mother in mannerism, style, appearance, and speech that he felt certain Mom could come up with no objection to her. And it worked! Mom loved her. Dad, on the other hand, couldn't stand her![77]

OK, it's a corny story. But it illustrates an important truth. Our perspective always impacts whether we see things as easy or difficult. If we expect everything in life to be easy, then nearly everything we experience will seem hard.

In the twenty-first century, people have begun to believe that life shouldn't be hard. Perhaps we believe this because of the advances in technology and all the modern conveniences we enjoy. But life has always been hard, and it will continue to be hard, especially for anyone who has goals and aspirations. Previous generations took this for granted and maintained a better perspective. That was true of a certain person with big dreams who persevered in American history. Here's what happened to him:

> When he was seven years old, his family was forced out of their home on a legal technicality, and he had to work to help support them. At age nine, his mother died. At twenty-two, he lost his job as a store clerk. He wanted to go to law school, but his education wasn't good enough. At twenty-three, he went into debt to become a partner in a small store. At twenty-six, his business partner died, leaving him a huge debt that took years to repay. At twenty-eight, after courting a girl for four years, he asked her to marry him. She said no. At thirty-seven, on his third try, he was elected to Congress, but two years later, he failed to be reelected. At forty-one, his four-year-old son died. At forty-five, he ran for the Senate and lost. At forty-seven, he failed as the vice-presidential candidate. At forty-nine, he ran for the Senate again, and lost. At fifty-one, he was elected president of the United States. His name was Abraham Lincoln, a man many consider the greatest leader the country ever had. Some people get all the breaks.[78]

Did Lincoln see his life as hard? Or did he see it as … life? I suspect he didn't complain about the hand he was dealt. Many had it harder; others had it easier. But that didn't matter. He dealt with what he needed to deal with and kept going.

The more we modify our expectations and embrace the normality and value of hard, the greater our ability to endure it and the more we will learn from it. When you have perspective, you don't expect to always succeed. You expect setbacks, and you know a failure doesn't make *you* a failure. It's simply one of a series of challenges you must face in life. And you keep going. You are able to embrace the words of a character named Lane played by John Wayne in the 1973 movie *The Train Robbers*. He said, "You're gonna spend the rest of your life gettin' up one more time than you're knocked down, so you better start gettin' used to it."[79]

"You're gonna spend the rest of your life gettin' up one more time than you're knocked down, so you better start gettin' used to it."

—SPOKEN BY JOHN WAYNE

The ability to embrace the value of hard is one of the most important mental shifts you must make in order to get a return on failure in life. How you make that shift is up to you. I like what Jim Collins and Bill Lazier said in their book on entrepreneurship. They wrote:

> Most of us get decked somewhere along the way in life, slammed to the ground, the world looking down on us. And when—not *if*, *when*—that happens, we have a choice. Do we get back up? And when it happens again, do we get back up again? And again, and again, and again, and again? When I'm feeling clobbered by events, pounded by setbacks, or just flat-out exhausted from dealing with my own mistakes, I think of Steve Jobs, Winston Churchill, and [legendary rock climber] Tommy Caldwell. Not persisting in a grim manner, full of endless suffering, but joyfully and gratefully persisting, fueled by passionately pursuing purposeful work. Life is way too long to give up early and way too short to be derailed from what we're passionate about and made to do.[80]

Often, I have to ask myself the *again* question. To put myself in the best position to get a return on failure, I need to not only say yes to getting up and trying again, but I also need to give that answer with joy and gratitude. To help me with this, I apply something I learned on a golf course years ago. I was playing a long uphill par-5 hole, and after the second shot, I was wondering how far I was from the green. So, I started looking for a yardage marker. Right in the middle of the fairway, I found one, and when I looked down to read what it said, it brought a smile to my face. The small brass plate on the sprinkler head read, "All you got." I pulled out my three-wood, hit the ball as far as I could, and still ended up a long way from the hole.

Later that day, after the round was over, that message kept coming to mind, and I thought about what a great metaphor that was for life. Continuing to learn, grow, advance, and climb uphill requires all we've got. We shouldn't ever expect it to become easy. In fact, as we get older, some things become more difficult. But that's OK. We never have to give *more* than we have. But if we continue to be willing to give what we do have, embracing persistence instead of the path of least resistance, we can achieve great things, and we will be content with the journey, having done our best.

DISCUSSION QUESTIONS

If you're reading this book with a group or as part of a mastermind, use the discussion questions to explore ideas, share insights and struggles, and grow together.

1. **Do you agree with the statement, "Everything worthwhile is uphill"? Explain.**

2. **How have the modern conveniences we enjoy today shaped our attitude toward what we consider hard? How do you think our attitudes compare to people one hundred years ago? Two hundred years ago? A thousand years ago?**

3. **How would you describe your everyday expectations toward life? Which way do you lean: Everything should be breezy easy, or everything you find will be a difficult grind?**

4. **What hard experience you've had in your life do you value most highly? Why?**

5. **In the most important area of your life, would you say you are in a season of sliding, plateauing, or climbing? Explain.**

6. **How do you respond to the idea that hard never ends?**

7. **Where in your current life are you sliding where you should be climbing? What will you do to change that?**

ACTION STEPS TO EMBRACE THE VALUE OF HARD

Take these steps from the chapter to get a bigger return on failure in your life:

1. Dedicate Yourself to the Idea of *Again*

One of the most important concepts we must accept to get a return on failure is that hard never ends. We must embrace the idea of *again*. Identify an important area of your life where you have given up but shouldn't. Commit yourself to going back to work in that area, create a plan to get back into the game, and then take that first step.

2. Go Down to Go Up

Identify an area of your life where you feel stuck. Maybe you need to make a difficult sacrifice of some kind to make the gains you desire. Examine the situation in that light to see what that might be. If the trade is worth it and it wouldn't violate your values, take action.

3. Change Your Habits Toward *Hard*

If you are not as tenacious and persistent as you want to be, then you need to choose different habits. What can you do differently every day to become someone who does hard things? Start small with changes you can and will do. You can begin anywhere: Start exercising, eat better, develop better work habits, clean the house, get more sleep. Once you've developed better habits and gained momentum, then build upon them to increase the difficulty and consistency of your actions.

4. Become a Beginner Again

One of the best ways to embrace the value of *hard* is to adopt a beginner's mindset. You can do that by learning something new, especially a skill outside your comfort zone. Study a subject that stretches you, sign yourself up for a difficult class, learn a new skill, or take on a challenging hobby. Anything that makes you a beginner and causes you to feel embarrassed will be beneficial.

6

Practice the Cycle of Improvement

If you want your organization, your team, and even yourself to grow, remaining the same is not an option. We know this because it seems obvious. Yet at the same time, most of us resist change. I'm sure you've heard this saying: The definition of insanity is doing the same thing over and over and expecting different results. We know that if we always do what we've always done, we'll always get what we've always gotten. Journalist and author Gail Sheehy wrote:

> If we don't change, we don't grow. If we don't grow, we are not really living. Growth demands a temporary surrender of security. It may mean a giving up of familiar but limiting patterns, safe but unrewarding work, beliefs no longer believed in, relationships that have lost their meaning. As Dostoyevsky put it, "Taking a step, uttering a new word, is what people fear most." The real fear should be of the opposite course.[81]

Many people fear change. They don't want to give up the familiar. Or worse, they are so stubborn that they defend what they *know* doesn't work out of pride or inflexibility. Mahatma Gandhi said, "Constant development is the law of life, and a man who always tries to maintain his dogmas in order to appear consistent drives himself into a false position."[82] I don't know about you, but I'd rather admit I was wrong, learn, and grow instead of insisting I'm right, remaining the same, and missing out on my potential. Besides, the more we grow, the more we will have been wrong in the past.

"Constant development is the law of life, and a man who always tries to maintain his dogmas in order to appear consistent drives himself into a false position."

—MAHATMA GANDHI

If, deep down, we want to improve, how do we keep from settling into our comfort zone? How do we break out of the rut that has the potential to make us crazy or create stagnation that keeps us unsuccessful? I believe the key is to develop a reset mindset. We need to find new approaches to the way we pursue success. We must learn to escape the trap described by former Vancouver Canucks coach Harry Neale, who is reputed to have said, "Last year we couldn't win at home and we were losing on the road. My failure as a coach was that I couldn't think of any place else to play."[83] You can find new places by resetting your thinking. I do this proactively by making sure that I am learning, unlearning, and relearning all the time. If you want to do it too, then you must start asking yourself three questions every day:

- **Learn:** What do I need to *learn* today that I didn't know yesterday?

- **Unlearn:** What do I need to *let go of* today that I held onto yesterday?
- **Relearn:** What do I need to *change* today that I was doing yesterday?

You'll notice that I used the word *today* in each of these questions. This is important. Why? Because asking these questions may be easy, but asking them consistently every day can be challenging. So can taking the appropriate actions on them.

THE CYCLE OF SUCCESS

To help you develop a reset mindset where you can learn, unlearn, relearn, and improve, I want to acquaint you with what I call the Cycle of Success. What may stand out to you in this process is that failure is necessary for success. It is assumed that you will take action that will fail, and instead of running from failure, you will learn from it. And one of the most valuable things about this cycle is that it can be used on a micro level on any given day, or it can be used for large business or leadership efforts. Here's how it works:

1. Test

The process starts with taking action because there is no progress or success without it. I like to think of this as *testing* because it removes hesitation. There is no pressure to make it perfect or to try to guarantee its success. People who say, "I must know before I go," don't test, and they often get stuck. Testing requires an "I must go before I know" mindset. As Tom Peters said, "If silly things were not done, intelligent things would never happen."[84] Testing may be doing silly things.

A testing mindset believes there is a better way. Finding a better way usually requires going *many* ways. Many years ago, I had a mentor who helped me with this kind of thinking. He often asked me, "When was the last time you did something for the first time?" If my answer indicated it had been a long time, he pushed me to take more risks. As your mentor, I want to ask you that same question: When was the last time you did something for the first time? If you tried something new in the last week or two, I want to affirm you. I also want to add another question: When was the last time you did something for the last time? In other words, how recently have you let go of an old way of doing things because it's no longer effective? Again, if it was recently, I commend you.

A testing mindset believes there is a better way. Finding a better way usually requires going *many* ways.

Being willing to start the success cycle by testing means that you must be OK with letting go—of preconceived notions, of past methods, of outdated beliefs, of whatever is holding you back from improving. I like a story Lloyd John Ogilvie told in his book *Falling into Greatness*, which illustrates this concept. He wrote:

> A friend of mine, a highflier in the circus in his youth, tells me that the secret of becoming a successful trapeze artist is in overcoming the fear of falling.
>
> "Once you know that the net below will catch you, you stop worrying about falling," he says. "You actually learn to fall successfully! What I mean is, you can concentrate on catching the trapeze swinging toward you, and not on falling, because repeated falls in the past have convinced you that the net is strong and reliable when you do fall. The

> rope in the net hurts only if you stiffen up and resist it. The result of falling and being caught by the net is a mysterious confidence and daring on the trapeze. You fall less. Each fall makes you able to risk more!"[85]

Many years ago, I read about a professor at the University of Houston named Jack Matson who taught a course called Failure 101, and I was intrigued because I love the idea of taking a class just to test ideas and actions, expecting them to fail. "Getting away from perfectionism frees your imagination," said Matson. His students designed hamster hot tubs and kites that would fly in hurricanes. The ideas were ridiculous, but Matson said, "Opening the door to the potential of failure taught students it's no big deal." In an article about Matson, Vic Sussman wrote:

> Once Matson's students equated failure with innovation instead of defeat, they felt free to try anything. Instead of dismissing ideas for fear of being ridiculed, students realized, "Hey, this came out of me," says Matson. "They saw they had the ability to take off in unknown directions and get rewarded for it. ..."
>
> Students also discovered the two ways to fail. One approach, trying out things sequentially, what Matson calls "slow, stupid failure," is the worst. The process is so drawn out "that you get worn out and say the hell with it." The other way, "intelligent, fast failure" means launching several ideas at once and readying several more for the next salvo. "Failure is a normal, natural way of mapping out the unknown," says Matson.[86]

Recently, I was given the opportunity to write songs inspired by the books that I have written. My friend Chris Oglesby, vice president of publishing and head of creative at BMG in Nashville, came up with this idea and offered me the chance to work with his top writers in his studios. What a dream come true! As excited as I was, I also felt nervous. My mind raced: *I've never done this before. … I'm in over my head. … This is going to be such fun. … I'm going to learn a lot!*

In preparation for my first session in Nashville, I sat down and began writing lyrics for a song called "Sometimes You Win—Sometimes You Learn." When I finished, I sent them to Chris to get his feedback. I hoped he would be impressed. After all, I have written a lot of successful books. But his response reset my expectations. He said the song was good—good for a first attempt. But it could become better. And he said it would get better when the writers and I went into the studio together.

The reality was that we started over again from scratch. Draft number one was a test, and it didn't make the cut. But it had enough ideas for the writing team to build on. And we rewrote the song. Six hours later, after many changes, tweaks, starts, and stops, we had a good draft—good enough to build on and improve even further.

The whole experience reminded me that nobody is good the first time, and, to paraphrase Ernest Hemingway, first drafts are always crap. You have to be willing to wade through crap during the testing phase of the success cycle if you want to get a good return on failure.

2. Fail

If you are willing to test, you will fail. That may happen most of the time. But here's the good news. The cycle of success is exactly that: a cycle. It's not a straightforward journey to a destination. Failure does not lead you to a dead end. It takes you to a temporary stop along the way on a journey worth taking, a journey that leads to success.

Some of the most innovative thinkers and organizations value failure highly and are actually intentional in producing it. Harvard leadership professor Amy C. Edmondson studied groups "strategically producing failures—in the right places, at the right times—through systematic experimentation." She explained:

> Researchers in basic science know that although the experiments they conduct will occasionally result in a spectacular success, a large percentage of them (70% or higher in some fields) will fail. How do these people get out of bed in the morning? First, they know that failure is not optional in their work; it's part of being at the leading edge of scientific discovery. Second, far more than most of us, they understand that every failure conveys valuable information, and they're eager to get it before the competition does.
>
> In contrast, managers in charge of piloting a new product or service—a classic example of experimentation in business—typically do whatever they can to make sure that the pilot is perfect right out of the starting gate. Ironically, this hunger to succeed can later inhibit the success of the official launch. Too often, managers in charge of pilots design optimal conditions rather than representative ones. Thus the pilot doesn't produce knowledge about what *won't* work.[87]

Inherent in Edmondson's comment is an implication that leads directly to the next phase of the cycle of success.

3. Evaluate

You've probably heard the old adage, "Experience is the best teacher." I think that's not true. Evaluated experience is the best teacher. If you have an experience, that doesn't mean you learned from it. The same goes for failure.

Failing doesn't have value—unless you evaluate it. That's why researchers such as Sim Sitkin, Duke University professor of management, termed some experiments gone wrong as "intelligent failures." Edmondson wrote about this. She said that there are areas where intelligent failures are not only welcome; they are necessary. "Discovering new drugs, creating a radically new business, designing an innovative product, and testing customer reactions in a brand-new market are tasks that require intelligent failures," she said.[88] Evaluation allows you to have intelligent failures.

In their book *Competing for the Future*, business professors Gary Hamel and C. K. Prahalad wrote about an experiment that illustrates the importance of evaluating your experience every time you fail:

> A friend of ours once described an experiment with monkeys. Four monkeys were put into a room. In the center of the room was a tall pole with a bunch of bananas suspended from the top. One particularly hungry monkey eagerly scampered up the pole, intent on retrieving a banana. Just as he reached out to grasp the banana, he was hit with a torrent of cold water from an overhead shower. With a squeal, the monkey abandoned its quest and retreated down the pole. Each monkey attempted, in turn, to secure the banana. Each received an equally chilly shower, and each scampered down without the prize. After repeated drenchings, the monkeys finally gave up on the bananas.
>
> With the primates thus conditioned, one of the original four was removed from the experiment and a new monkey added. No sooner had this new, innocent monkey started up the pole than his (or her) companions reached up and yanked

> the surprised creature back down the pole. The monkey got the message—don't climb that pole. After a few such aborted attempts, but without having received a cold shower, the new monkey stopped trying to get the bananas. One by one, each of the original monkeys was replaced. Each new monkey learned the same lesson: Don't climb the pole. None of the new monkeys ever made it to the top of the pole; none even got so far as a cold shower. Not one understood precisely why the pole climbing was discouraged, but they all respected the well-established precedent. Even after the shower was removed, no monkey ventured up the pole. We're not suggesting that managers are monkeys! We are suggesting that precedents, enacted into policy manuals, corporate processes, and training programs often outlive the particular industry context that created them.
>
> The second, and perhaps greater hazard, is that individuals don't know what they don't know and, worse yet, don't know that they don't know. This is the great challenge for every organization: How do we come to know what we don't know? How can we identify, and then transcend, the boundaries to our knowledge?[89]

If we simply react to every success by celebrating and to every failure by avoiding the actions that led to it, we don't gain anything. But if we take the time to evaluate carefully, we can move on to the next phase of the cycle of success.

4. Learn

There's an old *Peanuts* comic strip I love that shows Charlie Brown's friend Linus at the beach building a beautifully elaborate sandcastle.

As Linus sits in the middle of his creation, admiring his progress, a few raindrops begin to fall. Those drops turn into a deluge. Sitting in the pouring rain, surrounded by flattened sand, Linus utters, "There's a lesson to be learned here somewhere, but I don't know what it is."[90]

Unfortunately, that's the attitude of many people who experience failure, and it's the reason they don't get a return on it. Instead of learning from failure, they feel it. Fear, disappointment, embarrassment, and a host of other negative emotions cause them to disassociate from failure and disown it as quickly as possible. That's why the most important question to ask yourself in the wave of failure is, "What am I learning?"

Eric Hoffer wrote, "In a time of drastic change, it is the learners who inherit the future. The unlearned usually find themselves equipped to live in a world that no longer exists."[91] In other words, your only guarantee that tomorrow will be better than today is your commitment to learn from it. The ideas you had today will not be sufficient to solve the problems of tomorrow. You need to learn to become better equipped to face a new day. Each new level of life demands a different and better you to meet it.

"In a time of drastic change, it is the learners who inherit the future. The unlearned usually find themselves equipped to live in a world that no longer exists."

—Eric Hoffer

I love the advice of Microsoft chairman and CEO Satya Nadella. To put yourself in the best position to meet life's challenges both now and in the future, become a learn-it-all. He commented:

> [Say] you have two students—one of them has more innate capability, and the other has less. The person who has less, but is a learn-it-all, will ultimately [become] better. That applies to CEOs, and that applies to companies. I think it has been a helpful cultural metaphor for us to say that you can't act like a know-it-all; you have to be a learn-it-all.[92]

Every failure is a learning opportunity. The more you fail, the more you have the potential to learn. Each time you test, fail, evaluate, and learn, you develop what I like to call layered learning. We're almost never good at anything we do for the first time. Honestly, we're not too hot the second time either. But if we keep testing imperfectly and learning from it, the many lessons we learn from our losses will help us improve, layer by layer. Create enough of those layers, and you begin to have wisdom.

Adlai Stevenson II, who served as governor of Illinois and ran for the United States presidency twice, described the importance of learning from evaluated experience over time. Speaking at his alma mater, Princeton University, he said:

> What a man knows at fifty that he did not know at twenty is, for the most part, incommunicable. The laws, the aphorisms, the generalizations, the universal truths, the parables, the old saws—all of the observations about life which can be communicated handily in ready, verbal packages—are as well known to a man at twenty who has been attentive as to a man at fifty. He has been told them all, he has read them all, and he has probably repeated them all before he graduates from college; but he has not lived them all.

> What he knows at fifty that he did not know at twenty boils down to something like this: The knowledge he has acquired with age is not the knowledge of formulas, or forms of words, but of people, of places, of actions—a knowledge not gained by words but by the touch, the sight, the sound of victories, the failures, the sleeplessness, devotion, love—the human experiences and emotions of this earth and of oneself and of other men; and perhaps too, a little faith, and a little reverence for things one cannot see.[93]

When you try something new and it doesn't work, do you evaluate your actions and learn from them so that you change what you do next time? When you stumble and fall, do you evaluate what happened and learn so that you can benefit from the experience? Do you possess a learn-it-all mindset? If you don't, you may be destined to keep doing the same thing over and over while expecting different results! But if you do stop to evaluate and learn every time you fail, then you position yourself for the next phase of the cycle of success.

5. Improve

People who test, fail, evaluate, and learn put themselves in a position to improve. And trust me, learning alone without improvement is overrated. It's similar to having good intentions. In the end, good intentions don't *change* anything. But when you add improvement to learning, you can change *everything*. And here's the good news: I believe

- Every*one* can improve,
- Every*thing* can be improved, and

- Every *day* has improvement possibilities.

If you share that mindset, you open the door to many possibilities, and you will *always* get a return on failure.

When I moved my company from San Diego to Atlanta nearly thirty years ago, I became aware of Chick-fil-A, a Georgia institution. And I met the Cathy family. I was able to get to know S. Truett, the restaurant chain's founder. The company is privately owned, and it has expanded greatly in the last thirty years. Back when Truett was alive and still running the company, he and his leadership team debated going into significant debt so they could expand and surpass their competition. Truett was not a fan of that idea. I heard that he finally settled the issue by saying, "I am tired of debating over our need to grow bigger. If we focus on getting better, our customers will demand that we get bigger."[94] And he was right. Truett started the first store himself south of Atlanta, and today there are more than three thousand across the United States, Canada, and Puerto Rico.[95]

I believe what James Allen said is true for many people when he remarked, "Men are anxious to improve their circumstances, but are unwilling to improve themselves; they therefore remain bound."[96] When we fail, learn, and adjust, our focus needs to be on ourselves, on what we didn't do right, on where we fall short, and on how we need to change. When we do this, we separate ourselves from people who do not receive a return on failure because no matter how many times we fail or how many different types of failure we experience, we grow, change, and improve. When we improve, instead of wanting to *go* to the next level, we intentionally *grow* to the next level. That's what I've continually worked to do. Because my focus has been on growth for more than fifty years,

I've outgrown yesterday—and grown into tomorrow;

I've outgrown old expectations—and
grown into new expectations;

I've outgrown past victories—and
grown into present victories;

I've outgrown average relationships—and
grown into growing relationships;

I've outgrown what was—and grown into what could be;

I've outgrown success—and grown into significance; and

I've outgrown my thoughts—and
grown into God's thoughts.

And I've learned that growth's highest reward is not what we get from it but what we become by it. That's the reward I desire for you too.

"Men are anxious to improve their circumstances,
but are unwilling to improve themselves;
they therefore remain bound."

—James Allen

---

6. Reenter

All this work in the cycle of success leads to this: the willingness to reenter, to get back in the race and try again—only wiser and better prepared. Too many people become discouraged, and they quit because they didn't succeed the first, or second, or third time. As Thomas Edison said, "Many of life's failures are people who did not realize how close they were to success when they gave up."[97] Successful people don't give up. They take the cycle of success full circle, reenter, and test again.

I don't know how naturally tenacious you are. Maybe you're stubborn and don't give up easily. If that's true, I applaud you. But I also say, when you get knocked down, don't just get up and jump back in again. Get up, evaluate, learn, improve, and *then* jump back in. On the other hand, if you're someone who has been easily discouraged and has allowed failure to stop you from moving forward, use the cycle of success to create grit and momentum in your life. You can use this cycle of success in your personal life and with your team.

I've studied entrepreneurs, and all of them practice something similar to the cycle of success. They test quickly. They fail without letting it stop or discourage them too much. They evaluate their actions. They learn. They improve themselves and their processes. And they reenter the fray. That was true of Sara Blakely, Mark Cuban, and Jamie Kern Lima. If they can do it, so can you. And with that frame of mind, you'll be ready for the next lesson in getting a positive return on failure: learning to recognize the difference between good and bad losses.

DISCUSSION QUESTIONS

If you're reading this book with a group or as part of a mastermind, use the discussion questions to explore ideas, share insights and struggles, and grow together.

1. **What is your response to the idea of learning, unlearning, and relearning every day?**
2. **What do you think about the idea of using *test* instead of something like *accomplish* to describe initiating action? How does it change your approach to risk and acceptance of failure?**
3. **What is your answer to the question, "When was the last time you did something for the first time?"**
4. **Which step in the Cycle of Success do you consider to be the most important: test, fail, evaluate, learn, or improve? Why?**
5. **What criteria do you use to evaluate an action you've taken or initiative you've led? What other criteria might be useful for you to add?**
6. **What role does flexibility play in the ability to use the Cycle of Success? How flexible do you consider yourself to be?**
7. **Where would you be willing to use the Cycle of Success? How do you think it would help you?**

ACTION STEPS TO PRACTICE THE CYCLE OF IMPROVEMENT

Take these steps from the chapter to get a bigger return on failure in your life:

1. Reevaluate a Past Failure

Choose a past failed initiative to reexamine using the Cycle of Improvement. Define what the "test" was as well as the failure. Carefully evaluate the outcome of the test, how it failed, and why. Discover the lessons you can learn from what occurred. Identify how you could improve any processes to get better results next time. Determine the best way to reenter and try again, only this time with better results.

2. Deliberately Fail to Gather Information

Apply the wisdom of scientific researchers by doing something you know will fail so that you can gather information. With the help of your team, choose an initiative and plan a process that will test the limits and likely fail. Then, together, utilize the Cycle of Success to learn as much as you can from the experience.

3. Follow Truett Cathy's Example

Think of someplace in your work life where you are consistently falling short of goals or targets. Instead of working harder, think of ways you can improve your skills and processes. Put your focus there for a predetermined amount of time, and then examine your results for improvement.

4. Do Something for the *Last* Time

Based on what you've learned from the Cycle of Success, look for practices that you or your team are still following that are no longer effective. Make the decision to officially retire them so that you can use your time and energy more effectively.

7

Learn the Difference Between Good Misses and Bad Misses

Casey Stengel, who played professional baseball during the same era as Babe Ruth, later managed the New York Yankees during their heyday, leading them to seven World Series victories. Nicknamed the Old Professor because of his deep knowledge of the game and strategic mind, he reputedly said after a loss, "You gotta lose 'em sometime. When you do, lose 'em right." What I love about that quote is that it contains an insight known to people who are able to get a return on failure. All losses are not equal—some are good, and some are not. Knowing the difference is a game changer.

ALL FAILURES ARE NOT CREATED EQUAL

I'm convinced that most people think all failures are created equal, and that's a mistake. When you understand they are not, you will begin to truly appreciate the positive impact of the good misses on your life.

Bad misses move us backward. But good misses can move us forward when we know how to get a return on them. They can help us to fail forward so that we experience a breakthrough instead of a breakdown.

Take a look at these seven differences between good and bad misses. And as you read about them, think about whether you've been prone to the good or bad in each instance so that you can improve your ability to get a positive return when you make mistakes or experience losses.

1. Failure Discovered Early—Good Miss
Failure Discovered Late—Bad Miss

Imagine yourself hurrying down the sidewalk beside a busy street while talking on your phone as you rush to an important appointment. Without noticing, you step into something soft. What do you do? Would you just keep walking because you want to get to that appointment? No, you would probably look down to see what you've gotten yourself into. What if you discovered you'd stepped with both feet into newly poured concrete? Would you just stand there and wait for it to harden? Of course not!

Failure is like setting concrete. The longer you stay in it, the harder it becomes and the more difficult it is to get out. That's why it's important for us to quickly discern that we've failed, made a mistake, or experienced a loss. The sooner we are aware of it, the faster we can do something about it. A quickly discovered loss is a good loss, while an undiscovered and uncorrected one can become a bad one.

Professor Amy Edmondson has observed that in organizations, especially large corporations, employees often don't want to admit or point out failures, and the longer problems are hidden or ignored, the worse they can become. She described how this occurred at Boeing, which has been described as a "beacon of American aviation leadership for over a century"[98] but has experienced major difficulties in recent years. Edmondson wrote:

> Shortly after arriving from Boeing to take the reins at Ford, in September 2006, Alan Mulally instituted a new system for detecting failures. He asked managers to color code their reports green for good, yellow for caution, or red for problems—a common management technique. According to a 2009 story in *Fortune,* at his first few meetings all the managers coded their operations green, to Mulally's frustration. Reminding them that the company had lost several billion dollars the previous year, he asked straight out, "Isn't anything not going well?" After one tentative yellow report was made about a serious product defect that would probably delay a launch, Mulally responded to the deathly silence that ensued with applause. After that, the weekly staff meeting was full of color.[99]

Unfortunately, Mulally's efforts to change the culture of Boeing didn't succeed, and problems with the company's planes have led to aviation tragedies and loss of life. In contrast to the culture of Boeing, Edmondson points to Eli Lilly, the pharmaceutical company, which held "failure parties" beginning in the 1990s to "honor intelligent, high-quality scientific experiments that fail to achieve the desired results."[100] Since failure was allowed, expected, encouraged, and celebrated, employees were more likely to notice failures and communicate about them early.

My brother Larry is very successful in the business world. I've learned a lot from him over the years, and the two greatest lessons he's taught that benefitted me are these: First, all is well that begins well. He helped me understand that the success of a project is highly reliant on the setup. When we work hard on the front end and ask as many questions as possible in the beginning, we have fewer misses.

The second lesson? Cut your losses quickly. Larry has observed that most people become emotionally attached to a project they launch, and they allow their emotions to overrule their judgment. They fail to see what's really happening and *hope* the situation is better than it is. But the truth is that problems don't go away on their own. Left unaddressed, they lead to failure. If you look for what's not going right and deal with it quickly, you have a chance to change course, make corrections, and achieve success. But if you're realistic and realize early that something is not going to work out, you should cut your losses and move on to something else.

2. Focusing on the Benefits of Failure—Good Miss
Focusing on the Detriments of Failure—Bad Miss

If you ever read the *Peanuts* comic strip, you know that it addresses the subject of failure often. In one strip, Lucy approaches Charlie Brown on the mound and says, "Sorry I missed that easy fly ball, manager. I thought I had it, but suddenly I remembered all the others I've missed." As she walks away, she explains, "The past got in my eyes!"[101]

That can be said of anyone who focuses on the detriments of failure. When we become preoccupied with all the bad effects of failure, not only does that negative past get in our eyes, but it also gets into our hearts. And that keeps us from moving forward because we become frustrated and discouraged. That can paralyze us.

It's far better to look for the benefits in failure or loss. That requires people to embrace a positive mindset. Azita Alavi, one of my certified coaches who enjoys working with youths, recently wrote that finding the benefit in failure enables us to "keep attempting something great. Optimism," she observed, "is not limited to a few people as a personality trait. Optimism is a choice. And while it doesn't guarantee immediate positive results, it does guarantee that you increase the odds of finding the answer."[102]

"Optimism is a choice. And while it doesn't guarantee immediate positive results, it does guarantee that you increase the odds of finding the answer."

—Azita Alavi

In his book *Leaders on Leadership: Interviews with Top Executives,* Warren Bennis interviewed seventy top performers from numerous fields. None of those leaders used the word *failure* to describe their mistakes. Instead, they referred to "learning experiences," "tuition paid," "detours," or "opportunities for growth."[103] Those are fantastic ways of looking at failure. When you make a mistake, suffer a loss, or experience a failure, what can you observe about yourself? What can you observe about others? What experience did you gain that can help you in the future? What method of working can you now rule out because it doesn't work? What are you now free to do because your time is no longer occupied by that other pursuit? There are a multitude of positive benefits you can gain if you're open-minded about failure and are willing to look.

3. Learning from Failure—Good Miss
Fleeing from Failure—Bad Miss

Most people try to avoid doing anything that might lead to failure, and if they *do* end up failing, they run away from it and pretend it never happened. The biggest problem with that is people who do those things never learn from failure. Fleeing failure is a bad miss. Learning from it is a good one.

I recently came across the story of Todd Hoffman, the person who came up with the idea for a show called *Gold Rush* on Discovery Channel. Hoffman was experiencing a hard time during the Great Recession when he got the idea for the show, inspired, in part, by his father's foray into Alaska gold mining in the 1980s. What it taught him was that mining is an exercise in learning from failure. Michael Scott Overholt, who wrote a story about Hoffman, said:

> Gold mining, apparently, is also a process of trial and error. The average amount of gold mined in a year between 2010 and 2021 was 2,980 metric tons, a value of $180 billion. Sounds like a lot, right? Yet the average annual pay for a gold miner is around $50,000. Weighed against the rising costs of equipment and fuel, operations are prone to going belly-up. The key is developing a knack, a different mining method the competition might not know about. And knacks are learned from failure. …
>
> From a personal development perspective, Hoffman's philosophy amounts to a growth mindset where one identifies their values and believes they can learn what needs to be learned, provided they don't give up. "You cannot give up," Hoffman insists. "You have to keep striving, even when you feel like you're less than or you have missed the mark."[104]

One of the lessons Hoffman learned while filming *Gold Rush* was that it took a great toll on his family. After eight seasons, he stepped away from the show, even though he had created it. Having spent six or seven months away from his family each year to shoot the show, in 2018, he knew he needed to make a change. "It just [came] to this point where I need to take a step back," Hoffman said at the time. "I need to raise my family, I need to do something else."[105] He learned from that experience too. In 2022, he launched a new show, *Hoffman Family Gold*, this time shooting it with his family included. This shows that he not only learned from his failures, but he avoided some of them based on his experience. That's what I call getting a return on failure.

Facing your failures and learning from them instead of fleeing from them takes courage. Engineer and inventor Charles F. Kettering said:

> There are two kinds of courage. One is a spontaneous explosion of aroused instincts to meet some sudden emergency. The other is steadfast and enduring against repeated failures and rebuffs. It is what boxers call "the fighting heart," the will to come bouncing back every time one is knocked down. All pioneers need that kind of courage. … Failures, *repeated* failures, are fingerposts on the road to achievement. The only time you do not fail is the last time you try something, and it works. One *fails forward* toward success.[106]

I hope you cultivate that kind of courage so that you will take risks, face your failures, learn from them, and then risk again. That's what Michael Jordan did. He said, "I've missed more than 9,000 shots in my career. I've lost almost 300 games. Twenty-six times, I've been trusted to take the game-winning shot and missed. I've failed over and over again in my life. And that is why I succeed."[107] Don't let thousands of misses stop you from taking another shot.

4. Failing in Your Area of Strength—Good Miss Failing in an Area of Weakness—Bad Miss

Years ago, I came across this cute little story, and I've always loved it.

> A young boy was playing baseball in his front yard. The lad announced to his mother, who was watching from the window, "I'm the GREATEST HITTER in all of baseball!" And he threw his ball into the air and took a mighty swing with his bat. He missed. "That's strike one!" he called. "Still two more to go, but I won't need them—I'm the greatest hitter in all of baseball."
>
> He tossed the ball into the air again and took another mighty swing. The ball landed softly at his feet.
>
> "That's strike two!" he yelled. "One more strike to go. Not a problem for the greatest hitter in all of baseball."
>
> He threw the ball in the air once more, and once again he took a mighty swing. He swung so hard he spun around on his heels and fell down onto the grass. The ball fell nearby, untouched.
>
> The boy got up, dusted off his pants and cried out, "Steeeee-rike three! I'm out!" His mother called out, "Aren't you upset you didn't get a hit? After all, you're the greatest hitter in all of baseball."
>
> The boy turned to her and smiled. "No way! Since I struck myself out, I just discovered I'm the GREATEST PITCHER in all of baseball!"[108]

OK, I admit it. It's another corny story. But it leads to an important truth that all of us need to know if we want to reach our potential. If we want to be successful, we must know our strengths and focus on using and developing them, not our weaknesses.

Here's how this works. I'll illustrate the idea by using numbers. If you think about people's natural talents, traits, and skills before they're developed, and you rank them low to high on a scale of 1 to 10, then anything with a score of 1 to 3 would be a natural weakness, anything scored from 4 to 5 would be average or mediocre, and anything with a score of 6 to 8 would be a natural strength. Notice that I excluded 9 and 10. Why? Because nobody's *undeveloped* natural talents or skills score that high. Only *developed* talent can reach that level.

I've observed that people who work to develop their talents, traits, and skills can raise them by one or two points. Occasionally, someone who works extremely hard can raise them by three points.

Now, think about how this works. Let's say I focus my time and energy on doing something for which I have little natural talent. When I first started my career, I did everything as the pastor of a church. One of my tasks was counseling individuals and couples. I'd say I was a 2 at that. Every time I counseled someone, what do you think my chances of success were? Low. When you do something you're terrible at, don't you fail often? I did. I was always impatient, frustrated, and ineffective. I don't know who walked away from those sessions more discouraged—them or me!

Let's play this out. Imagine that I decided I would focus my life on becoming a better counselor. I would read hundreds of books, get a counseling degree, do clinical hours, and pour myself into counseling. How would that turn out? At my best, I would probably be a 4. Or if I were really lucky, a 5. I'd be mediocre.

Fortunately, one of my other tasks was speaking. Today, I'm known as a good communicator, but back then, I wasn't very good. However—and this is vital—I had a natural talent for speaking. I had good stage presence. People naturally liked me. I had a sense of humor and could make people laugh. I could tell a story. I had a good memory. Thanks to my father's genes, I had a good voice. And I loved doing it.

When it came to natural talent, I'd say I was a 6 or 7 at speaking. When I spoke, did I still make mistakes? Of course. I made a lot of them. But those losses were good losses. Why? Because each time I failed, I learned and improved. Because I had talent, I was able to figure out what I did wrong and correct it. I was able to build upon my talent and be way above average.

When you *must* do something you're not good at and you fail—well, that's life. We all have that experience. However, when you choose to do something you're not good at and you fail—and you keep doing it—you're wasting your life, and all those misses will be bad misses because you will never receive a positive return on failure. Instead, stay with your strengths.

5. Making Adjustments—Good Miss
Making Excuses—Bad Miss

Receiving a return on failure requires making adjustments. We can literally adjust our way toward success. Unfortunately, instead of making adjustments, many people make excuses. That's a bad miss. It's easier for a person to move from failure to success than from excuses to success. Why? Because the person who makes excuses fails to take personal responsibility, and lack of responsibility always ultimately leads to failure.

It's easier for a person to move from failure to success than from excuses to success.

Life isn't about what happens to you. Life is about how you respond to what's happening to you. Everyone experiences setbacks, losses, mistakes, failures, and tragedies. The question is what we are going to do in response to them. Are we going to take responsibility and make adjustments? Or are we going to blame others, our circumstances, the government, or society? If you don't see your responsibility for your failures, you won't feel the responsibility to learn, adjust, and improve.

Many years ago, singer, actor, and author Portia Nelson wrote a poem called "Autobiography in Five Short Chapters." It describes a situation so many people find themselves facing in life:

Chapter One

I walk down the street.
There is a deep hole in the sidewalk.
I fall in.
I am lost ... I am helpless.
It isn't my fault.
It takes forever to find a way out.

Chapter Two

I walk down the same street.
There is a deep hole in the sidewalk.
I pretend I don't see it.
I fall in again.
I can't believe I am in the same place.
But, it isn't my fault.
It still takes a long time to get out.

Chapter Three

I walk down the same street.

There is a deep hole in the sidewalk.
I see it is there.
I still fall in … it's a habit … but,
my eyes are open.
I know where I am.
It *is* my fault.
I get out immediately.

Chapter Four

I walk down the same street.
There is a deep hole in the sidewalk.
I walk around it.

Chapter Five

I walk down another street.[109]

As I was working on this chapter with Charlie Wetzel, my book-writing collaborator for more than thirty years, I told him I wanted to include this poem, and he told me a story. While he was in counseling in his twenties, his counselor read this to him, and he thought, *That's my life!* He immediately began making changes in the way he lived. Charlie overcame a lot and turned his life around.

That's what anyone can do if they're willing to make adjustments. In Nelson's piece, the narrator experiences bad misses in chapters one, two, and three because they fail to make adjustments. But at the end of the third chapter, they understand that their failure is their fault, so they learn, make adjustments, and avoid the hole they had gotten stuck in over and over. And as a result, in chapter five, the narrator walks down a new road.

None of our lives will change until *we* change. The good news is that we can. And failure is often our greatest opportunity to know ourselves for who we really are and make improvements to ourselves so that we can become who we really want to be.

6. A Failure We Correct—Good Miss Repeated Failures Uncorrected—Bad Miss

Have you heard the expression, "Fool me once, shame on you. Fool me twice, shame on me"? Well, here's a similar thought: If I fail at something once, that's a good miss. But fail at a series of connected things one after the other without making corrections? That's a bad miss. Why? Because I had the chance to correct what I was doing wrong, and I didn't take it.

Failure is often not the cause of our problems. Repeated, uncorrected failures are. In their book *High Altitude Leadership*, Chris Warner and Don Schmincke wrote about the detrimental impact of repeated failures:

> In mountaineering, rarely does the first error kill a climber. Death occurs when the third thing goes wrong.
>
> On big peaks, we tell clients that the first mistake they made was joining the expedition. They are now in an environment where things can go terribly wrong very quickly. If they are going to make it home alive, they have to be more disciplined, more giving and more humbled than ever before. Everyone has to scan the horizon. Everyone has to examine themselves and each other for signs of weakness. Everyone is responsible for their own safety and the safety of everyone else. They have to prevent the small mistakes from adding up to a catastrophe.

> Just as in mountaineering, business leaders make small errors almost daily. But how many does it take before the errors reach a deadly magnitude of bringing down a project or a career or a company? Both organizations and expeditions fail because a series of mistakes build on themselves—and before anyone notices. How many teams failed before anyone realized that the demoralized culture, increased customer dissatisfaction and hemorrhaging profits would combine into an inescapable landslide?[110]

No one can be sloppy in effort or excellence and expect to get a return on failure. To be productive and accomplish our goals, we must pay attention to our performance, recognize when we're making mistakes, and correct them.

7. Moving into Positive Action After Failure—Good Miss
Mulling over Negative Emotions After Failure—Bad Miss

Let's face it: Failures mess with us. They can get us down and cause us to become stuck emotionally. Even the most positive of people can want to wallow in their emotions and give up. In his book *The Double Win*, Denis Waitley wrote a story about Norman Vincent Peale, who has been called the father of positive thinking. Waitley wrote:

> He had written a manuscript and sent it to a host of publishers without success. With his stack of rejection notices piled high, he threw the manuscript in the wastebasket in frustration. As his wife reached in to salvage it, he told her

> sternly, "We've wasted enough time on it. I forbid you to take it from the wastebasket."
>
> The following day she made a decision to try another publisher. When she arrived, the publisher noticed that her parcel looked odd, unlike any book he'd ever seen. It was too big, bulky, and the wrong shape to be a manuscript. When he unwrapped the clumsy package wrapped in brown paper, the publisher discovered a wastebasket containing a manuscript that we have come to know as *The Power of Positive Thinking*.[111]

Though Peale had given up, his wife Ruth had not. As a result, the book did get published, and it was a perennial bestseller for more than fifty years.

When you experience failure, you need to acknowledge your emotions and process them. But then you need to move on. The best way to do that is to get yourself moving and take action. Psychologist George W. Crane said, "Remember, motions are the precursors of emotions. You can't control the latter directly but only through your choice of motions or actions."[112] The sooner you take action, the sooner you can turn things around. And remember, it's not where you start that counts. It's where you finish and what you get done along the way.

I've accomplished a lot in my life. That means I'm old. If you stick around long enough and learn how to get a return on failure, you can accomplish a lot too. And at this stage of my life, I have people telling me what I have done is amazing. I thank them, but I know better. I'm not as good as people give me credit for, and I don't believe my own press. I often see my greatest assets as my hunger to learn, persistence, and consistency.

If you want to go far and accomplish much and live an amazing life, then you need to do many things that are mundane instead of amazing. For example:

Practicing is not amazing.

Studying is not amazing.

Showing up is not amazing.

Trying is not amazing.

Asking questions is not amazing.

Changing is not amazing.

Working is not amazing.

Failing is not amazing.

Trying again is not amazing.

If you are willing to keep failing and experiencing positive misses, keep learning, and keep showing up, you will get a positive return on failure. And that is amazing.

But doing these things every day for decades with a passion for improvement and for adding value to others—that is pretty amazing. And here's what's even more amazing. You can do all of those things for however much life you have left. If you are willing to keep failing and experiencing positive misses, keep learning, and keep showing up, you will get a positive return on failure. And that is amazing.

DISCUSSION QUESTIONS

If you're reading this book with a group or as part of a mastermind, use the discussion questions to explore ideas, share insights and struggles, and grow together.

1. **What is your reaction to the idea that all failures are not created equal? Have you ever entertained the idea of a miss being good? How does that idea impact your thinking?**

2. **Do you agree with the statement in the chapter that optimism is a choice? Explain.**

3. **What criteria have you used in the past to judge failure? In general, what principle does the chapter suggest you use to judge whether a failure is a good or bad miss?**

4. **The chapter suggests judging quickly whether something is a failure. How quickly are you able to recognize failure? What could you do to speed up that process?**

5. **To what degree do you think past failures cloud your judgment as you deal with current challenges?**

6. **Why does a person need courage to face failure? When have you needed to summon courage for this? Explain.**

7. **How much do you relate to "Autobiography in Five Short Chapters"? If you identify with the story, what do you need to do so that you can walk down a new street in your life?**

ACTION STEPS TO LEARN THE DIFFERENCE BETWEEN GOOD AND BAD MISSES

Take these steps from the chapter to get a bigger return on failure in your life:

1. Color Code Your Challenges

Introduce the use of color codes to your team to improve communication, identify failure more quickly, and improve performance. Use green for good, yellow for caution, and red for problems. Be sure to applaud good misses and coach team members to reduce the number of bad misses.

2. Cut Your Losses

There is likely a project or endeavor in your life that is going poorly and you are *hoping* it will turn around, despite evidence to the contrary. Examine it to determine whether you should cut your losses now. If you can't identify a current effort in this situation, then focus on an endeavor you are preparing to launch, and decide in advance how quickly you will cut your losses if it isn't succeeding. Predefine the failure point that will trigger shutting it down.

3. Stop Developing a Weakness

Most people grow up being asked to improve upon their weaknesses. In reaction to a poor grade in math or English, they are told to study that subject harder. As adults, we need to break this routine. Think of a low skill area you are currently working to improve. Instead of developing it, look for ways to avoid using it, and instead, focus your attention on developing a skill where you have natural talent and potential.

4. Take Action to Process Emotions

To lessen the emotional toll that failure takes on you, make it a practice to process your emotions thoroughly. Then make whatever corrections are needed and take action quickly to get yourself moving forward positively again.

8

Lead Others Through Failure

My hope is that you now feel confident facing failure, dealing with it in a healthy way, using it to make you better, and getting a positive return on it. Does that mean you're done? No, not if you are part of a family, lead a team, oversee an organization, or have friends. In other words, if there are important people in your life or you lead others, you need to take one more step. You need to help others by leading them through failure so they can be successful.

SEVEN STEPS TO HELP OTHERS GET A RETURN ON FAILURE

I must admit, getting a return on failure gives me a thrill. I love to be challenged and turn what looks like a loss into a gain. But even more, I love to help others do the same. Few things in life are more rewarding than adding value to others so that they can make a positive impact. If you want to lead others through failure, I recommend you do it by taking these seven steps:

1. Have Up-Front Conversations About Failure

Leaders are responsible for being clear about the difficulties of the success journey for the people they lead. Up-front conversations create up-front expectations, enabling people to have a realistic view of the ups and downs they should expect on their journey. The less experienced the person being led, the more important and more detailed that conversation about future failures needs to be. And the sooner those conversations occur, the better. Why do I say that? There are three reasons:

Up-front conversations create up-front expectations, enabling people to have a realistic view of the ups and downs they should expect on their journey.

The Fear of Failure Is Highest at the Beginning

When we begin a task, our fear of failing is usually at its highest. Sometimes it can be overwhelming, especially if that task is new, risky, or high-stakes. Our minds can be filled with negative questions. Our confidence is very low. And if we experience surprises, they are usually not positive ones. That can cause us to get stuck. And as Roberto Goizueta said, "The moment avoiding failure becomes your motivation, you're down the path of inactivity. You stumble only if you are moving."[113] We need to help people avoid getting locked up by failure.

As a leader, I feel a strong responsibility to help people realize that their fear is natural and that they *will* fail—and that's OK. I want them to understand that mistakes are not fatal and failure is not final. When leaders let their team know that failure is expected and accepted, team members take greater risks and are more likely to be honest when they fall short. In addition, when the entire team understands that failure is normal and the leader supports them, they will be more likely to support one another too.

The Possibility of Failure Is Highest at the Beginning

Often I see people tensely preparing for a project they have never done. When I ask them about it, they usually say something like, "I've never done this before, and I want to do a good job!" While I applaud their desire to achieve, I feel compelled to tell them the truth so they can relax: Nobody is ever good the first time.

That's simply a fact of life. Every first is a challenge. Most of the time, we don't do well. When you started to walk, were you good at it? When you started to talk, were your words clear and fluent? If you ever tried to hit a baseball for the first time, did you hit a home run? Of course not! We are never good at anything the first time.

When I went to college, I received my bachelor's degree in theology. As I prepared to seek my first job as a pastor, my guidance counselor gave me great advice. He said to go to a little church in a tiny town where I could fail and make lots of mistakes—because that would happen—and the people would be kind and forgiving and I could learn in obscurity. I followed his advice and discovered in my first few months that he was right. I got a lot wrong. Why? Because most of what I did, I was doing for the first time.

The Likelihood of a Wrong Response to Failure Is Highest at the Beginning

The third reason I feel up-front conversations about failure are important is that we are most likely to find ourselves having a wrong response when we get started. That is when our fears are the strongest, and our desire to quit is at an all-time high. In fact, I recently read about a survey finding that 21 percent of Gen Zers have acquaintances who have shown up for a new job and quit on the first day.[114] Evidently they are doing what most of us *feel* like doing when we start a new job. We say to ourselves, "I'm not cut out to do this" or "That work is not my gift." But here's the truth: We never know if we are going to be good at something in the beginning, and new starts are filled with failures. Our best chance to get through all the difficult stuff is to know before we start that we'll be facing challenges. And that's OK.

If you're a parent or a grandparent, one of the best things you can do for children is to have up-front conversations about failure with them and encourage them to try and fail often. One of my favorite stories about being prepared for failure comes from the life of Sara Blakely, the founder of Spanx. In her book *The Spanx Story*, author Stephanie Wetzel, the wife of my writing partner Charlie Wetzel, wrote about Sara:

> When she was very young … Sara's dad set up an unusual routine of asking Sara and her brother, Ford, about their failures at the dinner table. After they sat down to eat, he would start the conversation with the question, "What did you fail at this week?" Whether they described a sports tryout where they didn't make the team, or a new unit in math that they were struggling with, he never expressed disappointment at their failures or mistakes. Instead, he acted pleased about every failure, offering them a high five and exclaiming, "Great job!" He only acted disappointed when they had no failure to share, so it soon became clear that failure was something he wanted to hear about. The more things they tried but didn't succeed at, the more their dad celebrated with them. And he always pressed them to tell the

> whole story about the attempt and the failure. And after they told it, he again said how proud he was of them.
>
> Early on, the children learned to come to the table with at least one failure to talk about. To be able to do this, they constantly searched for things to try and fail at. All those frequent unsuccessful attempts, and the dinnertime conversations that followed, gradually led to a reframing of failure in their minds. "My dad taught me that failure is not an outcome," Sara said. Instead, he taught her that failure should be defined as a lack of trying, or "not stretching yourself far enough out of your comfort zone and attempting to be more than you were the day before."[115]

If we can help others to expect and embrace failure by having up-front conversations with them, we will help them immeasurably.

2. Openly Share Your Failures with Others

Professor Mike Lehman, who has developed entrepreneurial courses and programs at the University of Pittsburgh and Lehigh University, observed:

> As professionals working in higher education—and entrepreneurship—the chances are high that we won't always get it right the first time around. We need to be better at sharing our mistakes—those unanticipated failures, those unbelievable flops, and those countless frustrations—as opposed to focusing solely on what's worked. This "failure collaboration" will allow us to learn from one another and, collectively, move the entire field of entrepreneurship forward.[116]

No matter what field you work in, openly sharing your failures with others is a good idea. It sets the right expectations for others, provides them with realistic examples of welcome behavior, and gives them permission to fail.

We need to be better at sharing our mistakes—those unanticipated failures, those unbelievable flops, and those countless frustrations. … This "failure collaboration" will allow us to learn from one another and, collectively, move the entire field of entrepreneurship forward.

—Mike Lehman

Early in my leadership career, I talked a lot about my successes. I was young, and I wanted to establish my credibility. I wanted to impress people, and sometimes I did. But as I gained experience, I realized I wasn't helping people. Then one day, I talked about one of my failures, and I saw the impact it made on others. While they couldn't always relate to my wins, they certainly understood and related to my losses. And when I told them what I learned, what I did to recover, and how I grew, they saw a path they could follow. And it helped them.

Today I talk about my failures often. I understand that it makes me more relatable. Since I am a well-known speaker, a danger always exists that the people I want to help will become fans. That's not what I want. Instead, I want people to see themselves as my friends.

The other reason I talk about my failures often is that it encourages others to stay in the game and not give up. I hope they think, *If he messed up that badly and he hasn't quit, maybe I shouldn't either.* I want to show them that no matter how many times I get knocked down, I refuse to have a victim mentality. Instead, I maintain a victor's mindset. I want them to embrace that too.

3. Share the *Whole* Story, Not Just the Highlights

Viktor Frankl has often been celebrated as someone who overcame horrible experiences as a prisoner in Nazi concentration camps and remained positive and optimistic through it all. In his book *Discipline Is Destiny*, Ryan Holiday wrote, "We remember Viktor Frankl today as an unflagging optimist, the unwavering believer in human meaning despite the horrors he endured in the Holocaust. And yet, there is a note he sent to some friends in 1945, just after the war ended." Holiday goes on to communicate what was in that note:

> I am unspeakably tired, unspeakably sad, unspeakably lonely. ... In the camp, you really believed you had reached the low point of life—and then, when you came back, you were forced to see that things had not lasted, everything that had sustained you had been destroyed, that at the time when you have become human again, you could sink into an even more bottomless suffering.[117]

The despair Frankl felt after regaining his freedom is a part of the story that's rarely told, yet it should be. Why? Because all of our journeys are complex. They take twists and turns. And the difficult parts are as important as—if not more important than—the easy ones. Helping others understand this prepares them to weather failure and come out on the other side.

The need to overcome discouragement is something nearly everyone faces—not just people who suffer great tragedy, as Frankl did, but also people who are highly successful. Take, for example, Fred Rogers, the creator, producer, writer, and host of *Mister Rogers' Neighborhood*. Rogers was highly respected and loved by children everywhere. He won three daytime Emmy Awards, plus the Lifetime

Achievement Emmy Award. He was inducted into the Television Academy Hall of Fame. And he was awarded the Presidential Medal of Freedom.

Despite a long and satisfying career, he had his moments of doubt and struggle. On one of those occasions, he typed this note to himself:

> Am I kidding myself that I'm able to write a script again? Am I really just whistling Dixie? I wonder. Why don't I trust myself? Really that's what it's all about … that and not wanting to go through the agony of creation. AFTER ALL THESE YEARS IT'S JUST AS BAD AS EVER. I wonder if every creative artist goes through the tortures of the damned trying to create? GET TO IT, FRED. But don't let anybody ever tell anybody else that it was easy. It wasn't.[118]

Knowing that others struggle with failure and doubt encourages us to keep going when we feel defeated.

I've often shared that it was my pleasure to be mentored by John Wooden late in his life. What a privilege. Wooden has been called the greatest coach of all time. His UCLA Bruins basketball team won ten National Collegiate Athletic Association (NCAA) championships in twelve years, recorded three undefeated seasons, and once maintained an eighty-eight-game-winning streak. Coach Wooden is the only person to ever be inducted into the NCAA Hall of Fame as both a player and a coach. What a great success story! But that's not the *whole* story.

John Wooden coached high school basketball for eleven years. During World War II, he served in the United States Navy. Afterward, he coached college basketball for another seventeen years before winning his first NCAA championship in 1964. He was fifty-four and had coached for twenty-eight years before he reached the top of the mountain.

John Wooden was one of my heroes when I was growing up and playing basketball. He became a hero again to me as I got to know him personally and learned from him. He remains a hero to me. The word *hero* can be defined as "a person noted for feats of courage or nobility of purpose, especially one who has risked or sacrificed one's life."[119] There can be no courageous acts without adversity. Easy times do not produce heroes. Difficult times do. And here's the good news: Since we all face difficult times, we can be courageous and become heroes.

There can be no courageous acts without adversity. Easy times do not produce heroes. Difficult times do.

4. Close the Gap for Others

Most people feel there is a great gap between success and failure, and they fear they will never be able to make the leap across that gap. If you're a leader, you need to try to help them. If you've ever seen me speak to an audience, you've heard me say, "My name is John, and I'm your friend." I say that because I'm trying to help people close that gap. I want to help others understand that success is within reach and they don't need to be perfect to succeed.

I love a story Robert Fulghum told in his book *All I Really Need to Know I Learned in Kindergarten*. A troubled man paid a visit to his good and wise rabbi, and here's what happened:

> "Rabbi," he said, wringing his hands, "I am a failure. More than half the time I do not succeed in doing what I must do."
>
> "Oh?" said the rabbi.
>
> "Please say something wise, rabbi," said the man.

> After much pondering, the rabbi spoke as follows: "Ah, my son, I give you this wisdom: Go look on page 930 of *The New York Times Almanac* for the year 1970, and you will find peace of mind maybe."
>
> "Ah," said the man, and he went away and did that thing.
>
> Now this is what he found: The listing of the lifetime batting averages of all the greatest baseball players. Ty Cobb, the greatest slugger of them all, had a lifetime average of only .367.[120]

A good leader, like the wise rabbi, lets people know that they don't have to bat 1.000 to be successful. Baseball players who are successful at bat a third of the time in their careers are worthy of the Hall of Fame. There's a standard in their field that falls far short of perfection but is still considered excellent. Encourage people to strive for that standard in their profession.

5. Redefine Failure to Help Others Change Their Perspective

One of the most positive things you can teach people to do is redefine failure so they see it in a new light or from a different perspective. Positive psychology coach Paula Thompson, who teaches leadership classes at Pepperdine University, likened this process to photography. She wrote, "Photographers move the lens around to get different angles on the same shot. We can similarly change our perspective or situation to see them differently."[121] Using synonyms for *failure*, here are five of the ways she says you can redefine it:

Think of Yourself as a Novice

Anytime you try something new, you are a novice. Think of yourself that way and adopt a beginner's mindset instead of comparing yourself to experts. That way, you will give yourself more grace and greater chances for improvement.

Let Go of Perfectionism

Perfectionists tend to catastrophize small errors and minor slipups. Instead of acknowledging the 99 percent that went well, many focus on their one mistake and agonize over it. If that describes you, let go of perfectionism. No one does anything perfectly. No artistic masterpiece is perfect. No invention is perfect. No performance is perfect. No book is perfect. No business is perfect. Accept flawed performance as normal.

Embrace Ambiguity

The world we live in is complex and ever-changing. And competing priorities have become the norm. The pull of opposite demands causes some people to shut down. Others ignore one set of demands and embrace another and become extremists. We've seen this in politics. But the healthier path is to acknowledge the ambiguity of life, where two opposite ideas can both be valid. When you can do that, you no longer see every situation as a win-lose proposition where someone *must* fail. Instead, you can seek win-win solutions that benefit everyone.

The healthier path is to acknowledge the ambiguity of life, where two opposite ideas can both be valid. When you can do that, you no longer see every situation as a win-lose proposition where someone *must* fail.

Accept Trial and Error as Normal

When Sara Blakely's father encouraged her and her brother to fail, he was teaching them that learning by trial and error is normal and good. Innovative people accept this. As Paula Thompson noted, "A core principle of design thinking is the idea of failing fast and learning from failure. This mindset embraces failure as a natural part of the creative process." If you can help the people you lead to understand this, you free them up to innovate.

View Something That Didn't Work as Simply Unfinished

Thompson's last piece of advice is a phrase she said she borrowed from poet Amanda Gorman: "simply unfinished." Thompson said, "Something that looks failed or broken may only be a misrepresentation of an unfinished process."[122] What I like about this is that instead of feeling that a failure is final, it leaves the door open to revisit whatever didn't work, reconsider how to fix or improve it, and work on it until it becomes successful.

Many of my books are in this category. Often, I will write a lesson that will be part of a book someday. Over time, the book will often come together. However, sometimes, it never does. That's OK. Writing is a process that requires many things to be successful. Sometimes, I don't have enough "things." The process is simply unfinished.

I'm sure you can think of other synonyms for mistakes, losses, and failures. Use them to help your team or family redefine failure so that instead of becoming discouraged or giving up, they keep trying and learn to get a return on failure.

6. Show Others the Bigger Picture

People who get tripped up by failure are often so focused on some aspect of failure that they lose sight of the bigger picture. As a result, they fail to return to the fight and never get a return on failure. By helping them regain sight of the bigger picture, you can help them get back into the game and succeed.

Some of my favorite stories of people who failed, lost the big picture, gained it back, and succeeded are in the Bible, and I'd like to share a few of those. Before I do, let me say that I am a person of faith, but I'm not trying to push my faith on you. If the Bible offends you, simply skip ahead to the next section. But I want you to know that you don't have to be a person of faith to enjoy these stories.

There is a passage of the Bible in the book of Hebrews that's commonly called the Hall of Faith. It describes the great faith of the great heroes of the Bible. Well, today I want to tell you about the Hall of Chickens. I want to share a story about four leaders who lacked confidence and were full of fear. But when they encountered God, they saw the bigger picture, and they were able to move forward in spite of their fears.

The first was named Gideon. His community was continually attacked by Israel's enemies, and he was hiding out when an angel called him to save his people. He responded by saying, "But how can I save Israel? My clan is the weakest in Manasseh, and I am the least in my family." The Lord's answer was, "I will be with you, and you will strike down all the Midianites, leaving none alive."[123] God was with him, and he defeated Israel's enemies.

Another was named Jeremiah. He was called to be a prophet, but when the word of the Lord came to him, Jeremiah said, "I do not know how to speak; I am too young." In response, God said, "Do not say, 'I am too young.' You must go to everyone I send you to and say whatever I command you. Do not be afraid of them, for I am with you and will rescue you."[124] God kept his promise, Jeremiah spoke up, and today he is considered one of the major prophets.

Solomon, the son of David, was made king when his father died, and he was afraid. He cried out to God, "You have made your servant king in place of my father David. But I am only a little child and do not know how to carry out my duties." In response, God said, "I will give you a wise and discerning heart."[125] And God fulfilled his promise. Solomon became known for his wisdom and has been called the wisest person ever to have lived.

Finally, there is the story of Moses. When God appeared to him in the desert and called him to lead his people out of Egyptian bondage, Moses responded, "I have never been eloquent, neither in the past nor since you have spoken to your servant. I am slow of speech and tongue." God promised, "I will help you speak and will teach you what to say."[126] God fulfilled his promise. Moses returned to Egypt, challenged Pharaoh, led his people to freedom, and taught them God's ways, which became the foundation of their lives.

What do all of these stories have in common? There was a bigger picture these human leaders did not see. They thought of themselves as failures, and they were afraid. God saw them as successes and encouraged them to move forward. If the people you lead are afraid or feel like failures, try to show them the bigger picture and challenge them to accept their role, do their best, and move forward with your encouragement and support.

7. Mentor Others Through the Whole Process

Most of what I have suggested in this chapter to help you lead others through failure has been focused on teaching. I want to encourage you to take that to another level by mentoring them through the entire failure process. What's the difference? Teachers say, "Sit down, and I'll tell you what you need to know." Mentors say, "Come with me. Let's walk this road together."

People do what people see. Demonstration has greater impact than instruction. As leaders who help others through failure, we need to spend less time in the classroom, which is the model of teaching developed by the ancient Greeks, and spend more time on modeling character, showing technique, and answering questions on the job, which is the model developed by the ancient Hebrews. Their method of teaching was built on relationships and common experience. It's what craftspeople have done for centuries. They take apprentices who work alongside them until they master their craft. Then they, too, are able to pass along their knowledge and experience to the next generation. By doing the job with their mentor, the student sees and understands that mastering any craft is a process filled with failure as well as success. And the mentor is able to assess the student's progress, show them their mistakes, and help them learn from them.

Teachers say, "Sit down, and I'll tell you what you need to know." Mentors say, "Come with me. Let's walk this road together."

Assessment is an important part of this process. In fact, the word *assessment* was originally used in the sixteenth century to describe the process of determining taxes based on value. It later began to be used as a word meaning "estimation." The word's origins go back to the Latin *assidere*, which means "to sit beside."[127] As a mentor, you sit beside the person you're leading and teaching so that you work together until the one you teach can do the job alone.

I believe that most people need a bit of help dealing with failure. They need good modeling, positive mentoring, encouraging support, and consistent leadership. Why? Because like us, they hope for an easy road through life when the reality is that everything worthwhile is uphill, and it takes great effort to succeed. Author, speaker, and coach

Larry Julian says that most people avoid pain and seek out immediate gratification. They want the easy way. He wrote:

> It's because by nature and calculated design many of us prefer the beautiful lie over the ugly truth. Most people want something that offers pleasure and satisfaction without the pain, effort, risk, and sacrifice associated with achieving a desired goal.
>
> I wish there were a simple answer, a three-step formula, or a handy tip sheet to remedy your pain or eliminate your difficulty, but quite honestly, that wouldn't resolve the real issue. Life's challenges demand your response, and that response defines your character and determines your destiny. Difficulty is an essential part of our story. It calls us to overcome, persevere, and share our story to inspire others.[128]

You can be someone who strengthens their character, overcomes failure, and perseveres to success. And you can share your story, encourage others, and lead them to success by showing them how to get a return on failure. That will not only benefit them; it will also benefit the team they're on, the family they're in, and the community they serve.

DISCUSSION QUESTIONS

If you're reading this book with a group or as part of a mastermind, use the discussion questions to explore ideas, share insights and struggles, and grow together.

1. **How responsible do you feel for communicating expectations to people to help them deal with failure? Explain.**
2. **How often do you have up-front conversations about failure with team members, colleagues, family, or friends? How has that impacted your relationships and their performance?**
3. **What has been your greatest challenge while trying to help others deal with their failures and mistakes? What has made that so challenging to you?**
4. **In the past, how have you helped others deal with their discouragement? What action has been most successful? Why do you believe it was successful?**
5. **Which of the following perspective changes in the chapter do you believe will best help you to coach others through failure?**
    - *Think of Yourself as a Novice*
    - *Let Go of Perfectionism*
    - *Embrace Ambiguity*
    - *Accept Trial and Error as Normal*
    - *View Something that Didn't Work as Unfinished*
6. **What is the bigger picture you can share with your team members, family, colleagues, or friends?**
7. **How will you change the way you interact with others to put them in a better position to get a return on their failure?**

ACTION STEPS TO LEAD OTHERS THROUGH FAILURE

Take these steps from the chapter to get a bigger return on failure in your life:

1. Help People Get Out of Their Comfort Zone

The chapter discussed how difficult many tasks are at the beginning. In response, many people stay in their comfort zone. Have an up-front conversation with someone on your team or in your family who seems to be stuck in their comfort zone because of fear. Communicate with them that it will be OK if they fail as long as they try their best. Win or lose, after they take action, debrief with them and encourage them.

2. Tell People How Close They Are to Success

If someone on your team or in your family seems discouraged, take the time to communicate all of the things they have done right and are continuing to do. Encourage them with the big picture and let them know how close they are to breaking through and succeeding. Follow up with them daily or weekly until they achieve success. Then celebrate with them.

3. Share Your Past Failures

Connect with people and encourage them by sharing your past failures. Tell them how they impacted you, how you worked through them emotionally, and what you learned.

4. Mentor Someone Through Failure

If someone you lead is struggling, come alongside them to give emotional and functional support. Stay with them, meeting regularly, until they have worked through their difficulties and come out on the other side.

CONCLUSION

The Future Favors the Bold

One of my mentors was Robert Schuller, the founder of the Crystal Cathedral. One day, he and I were talking about a potential opportunity that I was considering, but I was having a hard time making up my mind. I wanted his advice on how to make the decision.

"John, would you do it if you knew you wouldn't fail?" he asked.

"Yes," I replied.

"Then you do not have a decision-making problem," he said. "You have a boldness problem."

That taught me a lesson. The point wasn't that I wouldn't fail if I tried, because I very well could. The lesson was that the path of success is littered with problems and possibilities, losses and lessons, obstacles and opportunities. How will we meet them? Will we shrink away? Or will we be bold?

There are really only three types of people in this world: the won'ts, the can'ts, and the wills. The *won'ts* oppose everything. The *can'ts* never accomplish anything. But the *wills* accomplish everything. How do the wills get things done? They know how to get a return on failure.

Now that you have changed your thinking about mistakes, problems, and losses, and you have learned how to get a return on failure, you have put yourself in a better position to seize opportunities because you know failure can't stop you. While it's true that learning to get a return on failure doesn't make success easy or automatic, it does open the door to many other life possibilities. Have the courage to seize them. If you hesitate, think of these words by author Betty Bender: "Anything I've ever done that ultimately was worthwhile initially scared me to death."[129] If you pursue opportunities, you may fail, or you may succeed. But if you don't pursue opportunities, you will *always* fail.

The *won'ts* oppose everything. The *can'ts* never accomplish anything. But the *wills* accomplish everything. How do the wills get things done? They know how to get a return on failure.

Don't let the messiness or uncertainty of an opportunity hold you back. Google pioneer and former YouTube CEO Susan Wojcicki said:

> Life doesn't always present you with the perfect opportunity at the perfect time. Opportunities come when you least expect them, or when you're not ready for them. Rarely are opportunities presented to you in the perfect way, in a nice little box with a yellow bow on top. … Opportunities, the good ones, they're messy and confusing and hard to recognize. They're risky. They challenge you.[130]

But that's OK. You're prepared to pursue them now. And remember, everything we do has an opportunity cost, a price we pay to seize or not seize an opportunity. Seizing an opportunity costs us time, energy, resources, and money. It also prevents us from choosing other opportunities. But not seizing an opportunity has a cost too. You give up that opportunity and all the potential it could bring. Plus, you give up something else: all the other opportunities it would lead to.

As you move forward, I recommend you follow the advice of Richard Branson, who saw more than his share of failure early in his life. He said, "If someone offers you an amazing opportunity, but you are not sure you can do it, say yes—then learn how to do it."[131] That's bold advice. But the future favors the bold. Be someone who

- Sees Failure as an Investment in Their Future,
- Keeps Success and Failure Together,
- Gets Over Failure Because They Get Over Themselves,
- Uses Failure to Make Them Better,
- Embraces the Value of Hard,
- Practices the Cycle of Improvement,
- Knows the Difference Between Good and Bad Misses, and
- Leads Others Through Failure.

"If someone offers you an amazing opportunity, but you are not sure you can do it, say yes—then learn how to do it."

—RICHARD BRANSON

Keep doing these things, and you will keep getting a return on failure, keep advancing, and keep making the most of your opportunities. Do that, and success is inevitable.

About the Author

JOHN C. MAXWELL is a number one *New York Times* bestselling author, speaker, coach, and leader who has sold more than thirty-six million books in fifty languages. He is the founder of Maxwell Leadership, a leadership development organization created to expand the reach of his principles of helping people lead powerful, positive change. Maxwell's books and programs have been translated into seventy languages and have been used to train tens of millions of leaders in every nation. His work also includes that of the Maxwell Leadership Foundation and EQUIP, nonprofit organizations that have impacted millions of adults and youth across the globe through values-based, people-centric leadership training.

Maxwell has been recognized as the number one leader in business by the American Management Association and as the world's most influential leadership expert by both *Business Insider* and *Inc. Magazine*. He is a recipient of the Horatio Alger Award and the Mother Teresa Prize for Global Peace and Leadership from the Luminary Leadership Network.

Maxwell and the work of Maxwell Leadership continue to influence individuals and organizations worldwide—from Fortune 500 CEOs and national leaders to entrepreneurs and the leaders of tomorrow. For more information about the author and Maxwell Leadership, visit maxwellleadership.com.

Endnotes

1 Max De Pree, *Leadership Is an Art* (New York: Currency, 2004), 11.

2 *Webster's New World Dictionary of American English*, 3rd college ed. (1991), s.v. "appreciation."

3 "Small Business Statistics," Chamber of Commerce, accessed March 23, 2023, https://www.chamberofcommerce.org/small-business-statistics/.

4 Jamie Kern Lima, *Believe It: How to Go from Underestimated to Unstoppable* (New York: Gallery Books, 2021), 48.

5 Martin Luther King Jr., "Draft of Chapter IV, 'Love in Action,'" Stanford | The Martin Luther King, Jr. Research and Education Institute, accessed March 24, 2023, https://kinginstitute.stanford.edu/king-papers/documents/draft-chapter-iv-love-action#:~:text=Forgiveness%20is%20not%20an%20occasional,them%20that%20despitefully%20used%20them.

6 "The Performer Within—A Workshop by Educator Eloise Ristad," Town Meeting TV, accessed March 24, 2023, https://www.cctv.org/watch-tv/programs/performer-within-workshop-educator-eloise-ristad.

7 Eloise Ristad, *A Soprano on Her Head: Right-Side-up Reflections on Life and Other Performances* (Moab, UT: Real People Press, 1982), 2189 of 3195, Kindle.

8 Theodore Isaac Rubin, AZ Quotes, https://www.azquotes.com/quote/253450.

9 Paula Thompson, "What Is Failure and How Can We Make the Most of It?," BetterUp, August 18, 2021, https://www.betterup.com/blog/what-is-failure.

10 Amy C. Edmondson, "Strategies for Learning from Failure," *Harvard Business Review*, April 2011, https://hbr.org/2011/04/strategies-for-learning-from-failure.

11 *The Simpsons*, season 5, episode 18, "Burns' Heir," written by Matt Groening, James L. Brooks, and Sam Simon, directed by Mark Kirkland, aired April 24, 1994, on Fox.

12 "The Donkey Story," *The New Sesquipedalian*, April 24, 2009, https://web.stanford.edu/dept/linguistics/newsletter/v5/v5i22.html.

13 "Last Writing of John Wesley (a letter to William Wilberforce)," ePlace, 2012, http://place.asburyseminary.edu/engaginggovernmentpapers/10.

14 Rudyard Kipling, "If—," Poetry Foundation, accessed March 29, 2023, https://www.poetryfoundation.org/poems/46473/if---.

15 Bill Gates, *The Road Ahead* (New York: Penguin, 1996), https://www.oxfordreference.com/display/10.1093/acref/9780191826719.001.0001/q-oro-ed4-00012282;jsessionid=16B60CDA858D1E4E674C9B8E A4B27679.

16 Francesca Gino and Gary P. Pisano, "Why Leaders Don't Learn from Success," *Harvard Business Review*, April 2011, https://hbr.org/2011/04/why-leaders-dont-learn-from-success.

17 Gino and Pisano, "Why Leaders Don't Learn from Success."

18 "Jim Tressel," National Football Foundation, accessed March 30, 2023, https://footballfoundation.org/hof_search.aspx?hof=2373.

19 Napoleon Hill, *Think and Grow Rich* (Anderson, S.C.: Mindpower Press, 2015), 73 of 506, Kindle.

20 Charles Schulz, *Peanuts*, September 17, 1973, https://peanuts.fandom.com/wiki/September_1973_comic_strips.

21 Yoni Blumberg, "Einstein's Handwritten Theory of Happiness Sold at Auction for $1.3 million—Here's What It Says," CNBC, October 25, 2017, https://www.cnbc.com/2017/10/25/heres-einsteins-theory-of-happiness-which-just-sold-for-1-point-3-million.html.

22 John C. Maxwell, *Developing the Leader Within You 2.0* (Nashville: Harper Collins Leadership, 2018), 58–60.

23 Don Levin, *Eight Points of the Compass: Directing Our Children on the Path to a Better Life* (Bloomington, IN: AuthorHouse, 2009), 75.

24 Grantland Rice, AZ Quotes, accessed April 3, 2023, https://www.azquotes.com/quote/591906.

25 J. I. Packer, *A Passion for Faithfulness: Wisdom from the Book of Nehemiah* (Wheaton, IL: Crossway, 1995), 2609 of 3103, Kindle.

26 Tom Morris, *Plato's Lemonade Stand* (Wisdom/Works, 2020), 307 of 4528, Kindle.

27 Og Mandino, *The Greatest Salesman in the World* (New York: Bantam, 1985), 80.

28 James Russell Lowell, *Among My Books* (Boston: Fields, Osgood, & Co., 1870), 377.

29 Burton L. White, *Raising a Happy, Unspoiled Child* (New York: Fireside, 1995), 161 of 254, Kindle.

30 Brian Tracy, AZ Quotes, May 27, 2014, https://www.azquotes.com/quote/1352572.

31 Quote Investigator, June 1, 2019, https://quoteinvestigator.com/2019/06/01/worry.

32 Ernie J. Zelinski, *The Joy of Not Knowing It All: Profiting from Creativity at Work or Play* (Edmonton: Visions International Publishing, 1994), 123.

33 Zach Pumerantz, "The 100 Best Sports Quotes of All Time," Bleacher Report, October 25, 2011, https://bleacherreport.com/articles/910238-the-100-best-sports-quotes-of-all-time.

34 Edmondson, "Strategies for Learning from Failure."

35 Edmondson, "Strategies for Learning from Failure." Emphasis added.

36 Joseph Grenny et al., *Influencer: The New Science of Leading Change*, 2nd ed. (New York: McGraw Hill Education, 2013), 134 of 300, Kindle.

37 Charles Schulz, *Peanuts*, date unknown.

38 Peter Davison, "The First Three Poems and One That Got Away," *The Atlantic*, April 1996, https://www.theatlantic.com/magazine/archive/1996/04/the-first-three-poems-and-one-that-got-away/304572.

39 Philip L. Gerber, "Robert Frost: American Poet," Britannica, updated March 22, 2023, https://www.britannica.com/biography/Robert-Frost/Works.

40 Jeff Rose, "15 Cheat Codes for Life: Jump 7 Years Ahead of People," Due, updated February 24, 2023, https://due.com/15-cheat-codes-for-life-jump-7-years-ahead-of-people.

41 Lillian Eichler Watson, *Light from Many Lamps: A Treasury of Inspiration Selected from the Wisdom of the Ages—The Foundations from the Past for Happier, More Confident Living Today and Hope for the Future* (New York: Fireside, 1988), 158.

42 Ken Blanchard, *The Heart of a Leader: Insights on the Art of Influence*, 2nd ed. (Colorado Springs: David C. Cook, 2007), 27.

43 Ryan Holiday, *The Obstacle Is the Way: The Timeless Art of Turning Trials Into Triumph* (New York: Portfolio/Penguin, 2014), 72.

44 Henry C. Link, *The Return to Religion* (New York: Macmillan, 1936), 29.

45 Steve Jobs, "'You've Got to Find What You Love,' Jobs Says", Stanford News, June 12, 2005, https://news.stanford.edu/2005/06/12/youve-got-find-love-jobs-says.

46 Winston Churchill, AZ Quotes, accessed April 5, 2023, https://www.azquotes.com/quote/449083.

47 Glenn Van Ekeren, *12 Simple Secrets to Experiencing Joy in Everyday Relationships* (Oviedo, FL: HigherLife Development Services, 2009), 668 of 3322, Kindle.

48 Hal Urban, *Life's Greatest Lessons: 20 Things That Matter* (New York: Fireside, 2005), 196.

49 Harper Lee, *To Kill a Mockingbird* (New York: Harper Perennial Modern Classics, 2006), 196 of 324, Kindle.

50 Norman McGowan, *My Years with Churchill* (London: Pan Books, 1959), 138, https://winstonchurchill.org/publications/finest-hour/finest-hour-152/i-leave-when-the-pub-closes-half-a-century-managing-the-press.

51 Kara Leverte Farley and Sheila M. Curry, *Get Motivated: Daily Psych-Ups* (New York: Fireside, 1994), 21.

52 Mike VanHelder, "The World's Most Expensive Bird Books," Audubon, May 2, 2016, https://www.audubon.org/news/the-worlds-most-expensive-bird-books.

53 "John James Audubon," National Gallery of Art, accessed May 8, 2023, https://www.nga.gov/collection/artist-info.122.html.

54 Tom Popomaronis, "5 Battle-Tested Dale Carnegie Quotes That All Entrepreneurs Need to Remember," Inc., May 17, 2016, https://www.inc.com/magazine/202304/diana-ransom/the-sba-after-ppp.html.

55 Ugo Juliet, "How to Win Friends and Influence People," Book Analysis, accessed May 8, 2023, https://bookanalysis.com/dale-carnegie/how-to-win-friends-and-influence-people.

56 Jacob Morton Brands, *New Treasury of Stories for Every Speaking and Writing Occasion* (Englewood Cliffs, NJ: Prentice Hall, 1959), 126.

57 Richard Feloni, "Thomas Edison's Reaction to His Factory Burning Down Shows Why He Was So Successful," Business Insider, May 9, 2014, https://www.businessinsider.com/thomas-edison-in-the-obstacle-is-the-way-2014-5?op=1.

58 Brian Tracy, "7 Keys to a Positive Personality," YouTube, June 11, 2012, https://www.youtube.com/watch?v=GUtEeWPW37c&t=182s.

59 Brené Brown, *Daring Greatly: How the Courage to Be Vulnerable Transforms the Way We Live, Love, Parent, and Lead* (New York: Avery, 2012), 16 of 287, Kindle.

60 Mahatma Gandhi, *Young India* (New York: Viking, 1927), 7, https://www.mkgandhi.org/voiceoftruth/franchiseandvoters.htm.

61 Gloria Germani, *Mother Teresa: An East–West Mysticsim*, trans. Thomas Pullosseril and Sonia Calza (New Delhi: New Age Books, 2003), 186.

62 Oprah Winfrey, "Oprah Winfrey's Commencement Address," Wellesely College, May 30, 1997, https://www.wellesley.edu/events/commencement/archives/1997commencement/commencementaddress.

63 Reinhold Niebuhr, *Reinhold Niebuhr: Major Works on Religion and Politics*, ed. Elisabeth Sifton (New York: Library of America, 2015), 866 of 1218, Kindle.

64 “The Rude Parrot,” 1Funny, accessed May 4, 2023, https://1funny.com/the-rude-parrot.

65 Jay Coughlan and Larry Julian, *Five Bold Choices: Rise Above Your Circumstances and Redefine Your Life* (Racine, WI: Broadstreet, 2016), 73 of 191, Kindle.

66 Charles Schulz, *Peanuts*, October 5, 1985, https://www.gocomics.com/peanuts/1985/10/05.

67 Author and source unknown.

68 Gary Burnison, *The Leadership Journey: How to Master the Four Critical Areas of Being a Great Leader* (Hoboken, NJ: Wiley, 2015), 24 of 96, Kindle.

69 M. Scott Peck, *The Road Less Traveled: A New Psychology of Love, Traditional Values, and Spiritual Growth*, 25th anniversary ed. (New York: Simon & Schuster, 2002), 135 of 4403, Kindle.

70 Frank Tracz, “You're in Charge … Now What?” accessed May 17, 2023, https://www.k-state.edu/band/downloads/handouts/youre%20in%20charge.pdf.

71 Fred Smith, “Training to Reach the Top,” Christianity Today, April 1, 1996, https://www.christianitytoday.com/pastors/1996/spring/6l2034.html.

72 Richard Rohr, *Falling Upward: A Spirituality for the Two Halves of Life* (San Francisco: Jossey-Bass, 2011), 321 of 3289, Kindle.

73 James Clear, *Atomic Habits: An Easy & Proven Way to Build Good Habits and Break Bad Ones* (New York: Avery, 2018), 35 of 307, Kindle.

74 Hill, *Think and Grow Rich*, 67 of 506.

75 Author unknown, “Climb the Steep,” poem.

76 John Hope Bryant, *Love Leadership: The New Way to Lead in a Fear-Based World* (San Francisco: Jossey-Bass, 2009), 489 of 2508, Kindle.

77 Author and source unknown.

78 James S. Hewett, *Illustrations Unlimited* (Wheaton, IL: Tyndale House, 1988), 17–18.

79 "The Train Robbers Quotes," IMDb, accessed January 6, 2025, https://www.imdb.com/title/tt0070825/quotes/?ref_=tt_dyk_qu.

80 Jim Collins and Bill Lazier, *Beyond Entrepreneurship 2.0: Turning Your Business Into an Enduring Great Company* (New York: Portfolio/Penguin, 2020), 145.

81 Gail Sheehy, *Passages: Predictable Crises of Adult Life* (New York: Dutton, 2013), 499 of 547, Kindle.

82 "Government Constitutes National Institution for Transforming India (NITI) Aayog," Press Information Bureau, Government of India, Cabinet, January 1, 2015, https://pib.gov.in/newsite/PrintRelease.aspx?relid=114268.

83 Don Martin, *Teamthink: Using the Sports Connection to Develop, Motivate, and Manage a Winning Business* (New York: Dutton, 1993), 77.

84 Tom Peters, AZ Quotes, accessed January 8, 2025, https://www.azquotes.com/quote/1403398.

85 Lloyd John Ogilvie, *Falling Into Greatness* (Nashville: Thomas Nelson, 1984), 207.

86 Vic Sussman, *U.S. News & World Report,* Volume 108, 1990, 65.

87 Edmondson, "Strategies for Learning from Failure."

88 Edmondson, "Strategies for Learning from Failure."

89 Gary Hamel and C. K. Prahalad, *Competing for the Future* (Boston: Harvard Business School Press, 1996), 1090-1110 of 5457, Kindle.

90 Charles Schulz, *Peanuts*, date unknown.

91 Quoted in Stephen R. Covey, *Everyday Greatness: Inspiration for a Meaningful Life* (Nashville: Rutledge Hill Press, 2006), 216.

92 "Microsoft's CEO on the Power of Being a Learn-It-All," Next Big Idea Club, accessed January 9, 2025, https://nextbigideaclub.com/conversation-microsofts-ceo-on-the-power-of-being-a-learn-it-all/17851/.

93 Adlai E. Stevenson, "The Educated Citizen: An Address to the Class of 1954, Princeton University, 22 March 1954," *Princeton University Library Chronicle* 61, no. 3 (Spring 2000): 426–427.

94 Boyd Bailey, "Life Lessons I Learned from S. Truett Cathy's Funeral," Wisdom Hunters, May 24, 2017, https://www.wisdomhunters.com/life-lessons-learned-s-truett-cathys-funeral.

95 "How Many Chick-fil-A Restaurant Locations Are There?" Chick-fil-A, accessed January 13, 2025, https://www.chick-fil-a.com/customer-support/who-we-are/our-restaurants/how-many-chick-fil-a-restaurant-locations-are-there.

96 James Allen, *As a Man Thinketh*, 129 of 395, Kindle.

97 "Thomas Edison Quotes," Charles Edison Fund, accessed January 9, 2025, https://www.charlesedisonfund.org/edison-quotes-images#:~:text=Thomas%20Edison%20Quotes,success%20when%20they%20gave%20up.%E2%80%9D.

98 Christopher S. Tang, "Boeing's Organizational Problems Date Back Two Decades," Industry Week, February 8, 2024, https://www.industryweek.com/supply-chain/supplier-relationships/article/21282352/boeings-organizational-problems-date-back-two-decades.

99 Edmondson, "Strategies for Learning from Failure."

100 Edmondson, "Strategies for Learning from Failure."

101 Charles Schulz, *Peanuts*, July 7, 1989.

102 Azita Alavi, "Failure Always Comes First! Get Used to It!" The Center for Youth Leadership, September 22, 2018, https://center4youthleadership.com/2018/09/22/failure-always-comes-first-get-used-to-it/.

103 Warren Bennis, ed., *Leaders on Leadership: Interviews with Top Executives* (Boston: Harvard Business School Press, 1992).

104 Michael Scott Overholt, "Turning Failures into Gold: Discovery Channel's Todd Hoffman from *Gold Rush*," *The Jesus Calling Magazine* (Winter 2023): 21.

105 Jennifer Tisdale, "The Toddfather Stakes His Claim in 'Hoffman Family Gold'—Why Did Todd Hoffman Leave 'Gold Rush'?" Distractify, June 30, 2023, https://www.distractify.com/p/why-did-todd-hoffman-leave-gold-rush.

106 Charles F. Kettering, "Education Begins at Home," *School and Society* 59, no. 1514 (1944): 12, https://archive.org/details/sim_usa-today_1944-01-01_59_1514/mode/2up.

107 Michael Jordan, Forbes Quotes, accessed January 16, 2025, https://www.forbes.com/quotes/11194/.

108 Author and source unknown.

109 Portia Nelson, There's a Hole in My Sidewalk: The Romance of Self-Discovery, 35th anniversary ed. (New York: Atria Books, 2012), xi–xii.

110 Chris Warner and Don Schmincke, *High Altitude Leadership: What the World's Most Forbidding Peaks Teach Us About Success* (San Francisco: Jossey-Bass, 2009), 197.

111 Denis Waitley, *The Double Win*, (Old Tappan, NJ: (Fleming H. Revell, 1985), 154–155.

112 David J. Schwartz, *The Magic of Thinking Big* (New York: Prentice Hall, 1987), 67 of 309, Kindle.

113 Quoted in Shawn M. Galloway, "Is Failing Less a Better Safety Goal than Achieving Success?" *Occupational Health & Safety*, October 1, 2013, https://ohsonline.com/articles/2013/10/01/is-failing-less-a-better-safety-goal-than-achieving-success.aspx?admgarea=news&jw_start=.

114 Bruce Crumley, "What a New Poll Says About Gen-Z's Workplace Issues. There Are Many," Inc., January 29, 2025, https://www.inc.com/bruce-crumley/what-a-new-poll-says-about-gen-zs-workplace-issues-there-are-many/91140559?mvgt=bSx4UqW5MbA1&utm_source=newsletters&utm_medium=email&utm_campaign=INC%

115 Stephanie Wetzel and Charlie Wetzel, *The Spanx Story: What's Underneath the Incredible Success of Sara Blakely's Billion Dollar Empire* (Nashville: HarperCollins Leadership, 2020), 12–13.

116 Mike Lehman, "Failures, Flops, and Frustrations: Learning from Our Mistakes," Venturewell, February 14, 2017, https://venturewell.org/blog/failures-flops-frustrations/.

117 Ryan Holiday, *Discipline Is Destiny: The Power of Self-Control* (New York: Portfolio, 2022), 141 of 316, Kindle.

118 Maxwell King, *The Good Neighbor: The Life and Work of Fred Rogers* (New York: Abrams, 2019), 315 of 423, Kindle.

119 *The American Heritage Dictionary of the English Language*, s.v. "hero," https://ahdictionary.com/word/search.html?q=hero&submit.x=52&submit.y=24.

120 Robert Fulghum, *All I Really Need to Know I Learned in Kindergarten: Uncommon Thoughts on Common Things* (London: HarperCollins Publishers, 1994), 165.

121 Thompson, "What Is Failure?"

122 Thompson, "What Is Failure?"

123 Judges 6:14–16 (New International Version).

124 Jeremiah 1:6–8 (New International Version).

125 1 Kings 3:7, 12 (New International Version).

126 Exodus 4:10, 12 (New International Version).

127 *Etymonline Online Etymology Dictionary*, s.v. "assessment," accessed January 24, 2025, https://www.etymonline.com/word/assessment.

128 Coughlan and Julian, *Five Bold Choices*, 25 of 191.

129 "Betty Bender Quotes," The Quotation Station, accessed February 3, 2025, http://www.thequotationstation.com/B/Betty-Bender/page1.html.

130 "Susan Wojcicki's JHU Commencement Speech Makes a Splash," Hub, May 29, 2014, https://hub.jhu.edu/2014/05/29/commencement-wisdom-wojcicki.

131 Lynne Schrum and Sandi Sumerfield, *Learning Supercharged: Digital Age Strategies and Insights from the Edtech Frontier* (Portland: International Society for Technology in Education, 2018), 65.